Southern Grace

Recipes and Remembrances from The W

Southern Grace
Recipes and Remembrances from The W

Published by the
Mississippi University for Women Alumnae Association

Library of Congress Control Number: 2003104375
ISBN: 0-9729217-0-2

Edited, Designed, and Manufactured by
Favorite Recipes® Press
an Imprint of

FRP™

P.O. Box 305142
Nashville, Tennessee 37230
800-358-0560

Art Director: Steve Newman
Managing Editor: Mary Cummings
Project Coordinator: Tanis Westbrook

Manufactured in the United States of America
First Printing: 2004   12,500 copies

The publisher of this cookbook wishes to thank Bridget Smith
Pieschel, Ph.D. and Stephen Robert Pieschel, Ph.D. for permission to
utilize information from their 1984 book *Loyal Daughters: One
Hundred Years at Mississippi University for Women*.

.

Cover photograph: The Catherine Wilkerson Bryan Gazebo

Cookbook Committee

Chairman
Jennifer Katool, CCP, *Class of 1978*

Co-Chairman
Susan Rayner Puckett, *Class of 1975*

Art and Design
Liza Cirlot Looser, *Class of 1980*

Marketing
Emily T. Myers, *Class of 1995*
Alma Coign Ellis, *Class of 1975*
Susan Rayner Puckett, *Class of 1975*

Fundraising
Lynne Curtis, *Class of 1970*
Gail Ferguson Laws, *Class of 1997*
Patsy Lockhart McDaniel, *Class of 1963*
Jennifer Katool, CCP, *Class of 1978*

Non-Recipe Text Researched and Written by
Susan Rayner Puckett, *Class of 1975*
Barbara White, *Class of 1975*

Recipes tested by
Sarah R. Labensky, CCP
Director, MUW Culinary Arts Institute

Advisors
Patsy Lockhart McDaniel, *Class of 1963*
Gail Ferguson Laws, *Class of 1997*

Photographer
Tom Joynt

Prop and Food Stylist
Mary Goodson

Foreword by Fannie Flagg

As an honorary alumna and friend of Mississippi University for Women, as well as a lover of good Southern food, I am thrilled to have been asked to write the foreword to this beautiful and delightful book!

Being from Alabama, I have been asked many times to try to explain what makes Southerners so different from people in the rest of the country. A hard question indeed, but I believe the answer lies in the rich culture in which we were reared, and a large part of that culture is food.

I know when I first left the South and moved to New York, after every visit home I always returned to New York carrying a container of my mother's homemade turnip greens, black-eyed peas, and cornbread on my lap just to take "a little bit of home" with me.

Throughout the years, many of us have stayed home, and some of us have scattered all across the world. No matter where you are, I know you, like I, will find *Southern Grace* to be a wonderful "little bit of home" filled with the memories and history of MUW, words of wisdom, and delicious recipes prepared just for you.

Benefactors

Grand Patrons
Nancy McClanahan Imes
Eugenia Summer

Patrons
The Family of Catherine Wilkerson Bryan
The Cirlot Agency
Joynt Photography
Jennifer Katool
Tom and Connie Sills Kossen
Carolyn Vance Smith
Leslie Farrell Threadgill

Sponsors
Linda Ross Aldy
AmSouth Bank
Larry and Kay Cobb
Columbus Bank Association
Lynne Bryson Curtis
Carol Puckett Daily
Chance and Gail Laws
National Bank of Commerce
River Oakes Health System
Sanderson Farms, Inc.
Trustmark
Vertex Aerospace LLC
Bill and Nancy Yates

Introduction

Mississippi University for Women (affectionately called The W by students, alumnae, and friends) was chartered in 1884 and made educational history as the first state-supported college for women in America. Originally known as the Industrial Institute and College (II&C), this institution was created by the Mississippi legislature to provide a high quality collegiate education for women coupled with practical vocational training.

The first session began with 341 girls in October 1885 in Columbus, Mississippi. The city of Columbus had acquired the college by virtue of its early interest in women's education and its willingness to commit financially to the endeavor by donating the buildings and grounds of the Columbus Female Institute, a private school founded in 1847. The first II&C class was graduated in 1889.

In 1920 the Industrial Institute and College became Mississippi State College for Women. By 1974 graduate programs had been added and MSCW became Mississippi University for Women. Men were admitted to the university in 1982, but MUW still provides a high quality liberal arts education with a distinct emphasis on professional development and leadership opportunities for women.

In its 2003 guide "America's Best Colleges," *U.S. News and World Report* ranked MUW as the best value among all Southern masters' universities. It is the sixth time in nine years that The W has been ranked a "best value" or "best buy" by this prestigious organization and further documents the quality of MUW. Well known for its beautiful campus and many historic buildings, The W has provided a rich educational experience for generations of young women.

Table of Contents

Appetizers and Beverages

Poindexter Hall

The Clock Tower

The chimes from The Clock Tower have been heard across the Mississippi University for Women campus since its inception in 1884. The imposing tower rises above Old Main Dormitory, the oldest building on campus, which was completed in 1860. Old Main Dormitory was closed for restoration in 1931 and reopened in 1938 as Callaway Hall in honor of Miss Mary Callaway, first "Mistress of Mathematics" and former acting president. Stories have spread down through the generations of students that The Clock Tower is haunted by the ghost of Miss Mary Callaway, whose heart, they believe, was broken by a young Civil War soldier.

The Clock Tower was partially destroyed in 1992 by a tornado. During the restoration that followed, the face of the clock was temporarily replaced by a round smiley face complete with mortarboard, putting a bright face on otherwise devastating tornado damage. The illuminated Clock Tower has become the W's best-known landmark, and its gentle chimes continue to serve as a welcome to Mississippi University for Women.

Phyllo Star Clusters with Caramelized Onions

2 tablespoons butter
1¹/₂ cups chopped onions
³/₄ cup chopped mushrooms
¹/₃ cup chopped roasted red pepper
2 tablespoons chopped black olives
¹/₄ teaspoon salt
12 sheets phyllo dough, thawed
¹/₂ cup (1 stick) butter, melted
4 ounces boursin cheese, softened

Melt 2 tablespoons butter in a skillet over medium heat. Add the onions and sauté for 4 to 7 minutes or until golden brown. Add the mushrooms, roasted red pepper, olives and salt and sauté lightly. Remove from the heat and let cool.

Unfold the phyllo dough and place between damp towels to prevent drying. Remove 1 sheet and place on a dry work surface. Brush lightly with melted butter. Top with another sheet and brush with butter. Repeat with 2 more sheets, making a stack of 4 sheets.

Cut the layered phyllo into 4-inch squares with a sharp knife. Place 1 rounded teaspoon of the onion filling in the center of each square and top with 1 teaspoon of the cheese. Pull the 4 corners of the pastry together and pinch and twist to seal. Place on an ungreased baking sheet. Repeat with the remaining phyllo dough, filling and cheese. Bake at 350 degrees for 16 to 18 minutes or until golden brown. Serve warm.

Yield: 18 clusters

Photograph for this recipe appears on page 8.

Brie and Grape Tartlets

1 cup seedless red grapes, halved
1/4 teaspoon kosher salt
2 tablespoons finely chopped green onion tops
1 tablespoon balsamic vinegar
2 teaspoons walnut oil
1/4 teaspoon chopped fresh rosemary
1/4 teaspoon minced garlic
1/8 teaspoon pepper
8 ounces ripe Brie cheese, chilled
48 appetizer-size puff pastry shells, baked
1/2 cup walnuts, toasted and chopped

Combine the grapes and salt in a food processor and pulse until the grapes are coarsely chopped. Remove to a mesh strainer and let drain for 10 minutes. Mix the green onions, vinegar, walnut oil, rosemary, garlic and pepper in a bowl. Add the grapes and mix well.

Cut the rind from the Brie using a sharp knife, being careful not to remove too much of the cheese. Cut the cheese into 48 cubes.

Arrange the puff pastry shells on a baking sheet. Fill each with 1/2 teaspoon of the walnuts and 1 cube of the cheese and top with 1/2 teaspoon of the grape mixture. Bake at 300 degrees for 5 minutes or until the cheese begins to melt. Serve immediately.

Yield: 48 tartlets

12

"Sometimes there are special places where special things happen. MUW is one of those places, rich in history and tradition. While our student population today is different from that of 1885 or 1930 or even 1990, it is still composed of strong students who take advantage of our first-rate academic programs and make us proud of them. When they return to visit, they often talk about the transformational effect that their educations had on their lives and how fortunate they feel to have been part of MUW. For our part, we feel equally blessed to have had them with us."

Claudia A. Limbert, Ph.D.
President, Mississippi University for Women

Broccoli Cheese Strudel

1/4 cup (1/2 stick) butter
1/4 cup all-purpose flour
1/2 teaspoon salt
1/4 teaspoon cayenne pepper
11/4 cups milk
4 ounces Swiss cheese, shredded
1 (10-ounce) package frozen broccoli florets, thawed,
    drained and chopped
8 ounces phyllo dough, thawed
1/4 cup (1/2 stick) butter, melted
1/4 cup bread crumbs

Melt 1/4 cup butter in a 2-quart saucepan over low heat. Stir
in the flour, salt and cayenne pepper. Add the milk gradually and
cook until thickened and smooth, stirring constantly. Add the
cheese and broccoli and cook until the cheese melts, stirring
constantly. Remove from the heat.

Overlap 2 sheets of the phyllo dough on waxed paper to
make a 12×20-inch rectangle. Brush lightly with melted butter.
Sprinkle with 1 tablespoon of the bread crumbs. Repeat with the
remaining phyllo, most of the melted butter and the bread crumbs
to make 6 layers. Spread the broccoli mixture evenly over half the
rectangle. Roll up as for a jelly roll, starting with the long side.

Place seam side down on a large baking sheet. Brush with
the remaining melted butter. Bake at 375 degrees for 30 minutes
or until golden brown. Remove to a wire rack and let cool for
11/2 hours. Cut into 1-inch slices and serve.

Yield: 6 servings

Arkansas Spinach Rockefeller

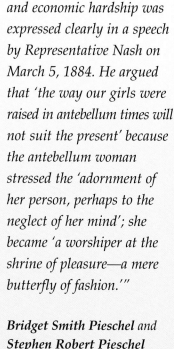

1 (10-ounce) package frozen chopped spinach, cooked,
    drained and squeezed dry
1/2 cup milk
1/2 cup (2 ounces) cubed sharp Cheddar cheese
Juice of 1 lemon
6 green onions, chopped
4 ounces mushrooms, sliced
1/4 cup chopped pimentos, drained well
2 tablespoons butter
1 teaspoon Tabasco sauce
1 teaspoon salt
1 egg, beaten
1/4 cup (1 ounce) grated Parmesan cheese

Combine the spinach, milk, Cheddar cheese, lemon juice, green onions, mushrooms, pimentos, butter, Tabasco sauce and salt in a saucepan. Cook over medium heat until the cheese melts, stirring occasionally. Remove from the heat.

Stir a small amount of the hot spinach mixture into the beaten egg in a small bowl. Pour the egg mixture into the saucepan and stir to mix well. Spoon into small buttered ramekins. Sprinkle with the Parmesan cheese. Bake at 350 degrees for 20 minutes or until the surface is bubbly and golden brown.

Yield: 4 to 6 servings

"The potential value of a women's college in an era of tremendous social change and economic hardship was expressed clearly in a speech by Representative Nash on March 5, 1884. He argued that 'the way our girls were raised in antebellum times will not suit the present' because the antebellum woman stressed the 'adornment of her person, perhaps to the neglect of her mind'; she became 'a worshiper at the shrine of pleasure—a mere butterfly of fashion.'"

Bridget Smith Pieschel and **Stephen Robert Pieschel** *in* Loyal Daughters

Zesty Pecans

1 tablespoon butter, melted
1/8 teaspoon cayenne pepper
1/8 teaspoon cinnamon
1/2 teaspoon salt
2 to 4 drops of Tabasco sauce
1 tablespoon Worcestershire sauce
1 cup pecan halves

Mix the melted butter, cayenne pepper, cinnamon, salt, Tabasco sauce and Worcestershire sauce in a bowl. Add the pecans and stir well to coat. Spread the pecans on a baking sheet and bake at 300 degrees for 10 minutes. Toss the pecans with a spatula. Bake for 5 to 10 minutes longer. Remove from the baking sheet and let cool.

Yield: 1 cup

Cheesy Cocktail Muffins

1 cup (2 sticks) butter, melted
8 ounces sharp Cheddar cheese, shredded
2 tablespoons chopped chives (optional)
1 cup sour cream
2 cups self-rising flour
Pinch of salt
Pinch of cayenne pepper
3 slices bacon, crisp-cooked and crumbled

Mix the melted butter and cheese in a bowl. Let cool for 2 minutes. Stir in the chives and sour cream. Add the flour and mix well. Stir in the salt, cayenne pepper and bacon. Fill greased miniature muffin cups 2/3 full with the batter. Bake at 375 degrees for 15 to 20 minutes or until a wooden pick inserted in the center comes out clean. Remove to a wire rack to cool.

Yield: 18 miniature muffins

Southern Grace

*Her voice is like the
    whisper of a warm wind
    through the pines
Her smile can reach
    the soul of any man
Her heart is strong,
    her love is true
And her touch is soft as lace
There ain't nothing
    like a woman
    with Southern Grace.*

*Little Texas
from their 1994 song*

Stuffed Mushrooms

16 large mushrooms, cleaned
2 tablespoons olive oil
6 ounces sweet Italian sausage, casings removed
1 garlic clove, minced
2 tablespoons finely chopped parsley
$1/4$ cup (1 ounce) grated Parmesan cheese
$1/4$ cup water
1 tablespoon olive oil

Remove the stems from the mushrooms and chop the stems. Heat 2 tablespoons olive oil in a skillet. Add the chopped mushroom stems, sausage and garlic and sauté until the sausage is cooked through. Remove from the heat and stir in the parsley and cheese.

Stuff the mushroom caps with the sausage mixture. Pour the water and 1 tablespoon olive oil into a baking dish. Place the mushrooms stuffed side up in the baking dish. Bake at 350 degrees for 20 minutes.

Yield: 16 mushrooms

The MUW Culinary Arts Institute, founded in 1996 and housed in historic Shattuck Hall, offers culinary training using classic cooking techniques as well as courses in entrepreneurship and small business development, food journalism, food art, and nutrition wellness. Students may choose to earn a Bachelor of Science degree in Culinary Arts, or they may opt for a certificate program or a minor in the field.

Mississippi Cheese Straws

1 cup all-purpose flour
$1/2$ teaspoon salt
$1/4$ teaspoon cayenne pepper
$1/4$ cup ($1/2$ stick) chilled butter
1 cup (4 ounces) shredded Cheddar cheese
1 egg
2 tablespoons water

Sift the flour, salt and cayenne pepper into a bowl. Cut in the butter and cheese with a pastry blender or fork. Beat the egg and water in a small bowl. Add to the flour mixture and knead into a stiff dough. Roll or pipe the dough into $1/2 \times 5$-inch strips and place on a baking sheet. Bake at 350 degrees for 15 minutes or until golden brown. Remove to a wire rack to cool.

Yield: 24 cheese straws

Variation:
Wrap the dough around jumbo stuffed olives and bake until golden brown.

Cora Mae's Cheese Straws

$10^2/3$ tablespoons ($1^1/3$ sticks) butter or margarine, softened
8 ounces extra-sharp Cheddar cheese, shredded
2 cups all-purpose flour
1 tablespoon water
$1/2$ teaspoon cayenne pepper

Cream the butter and cheese in a mixing bowl until well mixed. Beat in the flour, water and cayenne pepper to form a dough. Place in a cookie press fitted with a star tip. Press onto an ungreased baking sheet. Bake at 275 degrees for 30 minutes. Turn off the heat and leave the straws in the oven for 15 minutes longer to crisp. Remove to a wire rack to cool.

Yield: 48 cheese straws

Two cheese straw recipes? Yes, two. Mississippians love cheese straws, and every hostess has her favorite, usually made from an old family recipe. We received and tested many variations and just couldn't decide. These two are similar, but different. Always feel free to adjust the amount of cayenne pepper and the sharpness of the cheese to suit yourself.

Spanish Salsa

2 cucumbers, chopped
1 green bell pepper, chopped
3 large tomatoes, peeled and chopped
1 medium red onion, chopped
1 (15-ounce) can yellow corn, drained
4 ounces black olives, chopped
1/2 cup tomato sauce
2 jalapeño chiles, seeded and finely chopped
2 garlic cloves, minced
Juice of 2 limes
2 tablespoons chopped fresh cilantro
1 teaspoon each cayenne pepper and black pepper
Salt to taste

Combine all the ingredients in a large bowl and toss to mix well. Cover and chill thoroughly. Serve as a dip with corn chips or as a topping for grilled fish or chicken.

Yield: 4 cups

Picante Sauce

4 large tomatoes, peeled and chopped
1 large onion, chopped
1 large bell pepper, chopped
3 jalapeño chiles, seeded and finely chopped
2 garlic cloves, minced
1/4 cup vinegar
2 teaspoons dried cilantro
1 teaspoon each dried oregano and cayenne pepper
1/2 teaspoon salt
Juice of 1 lime

Combine all the ingredients in a large nonreactive saucepan. Cook over medium heat for 30 minutes, stirring occasionally. Purée in a food processor or blender. Serve warm as a topping for baked fish or chicken or chilled as a dip for raw vegetables or chips.

Yield: 4 cups

Bacon Artichoke Dip

1 (14-ounce) can artichoke hearts, well drained and chopped
1 cup sour cream
$1/2$ cup mayonnaise
$3/4$ cup frozen chopped spinach, thawed and well drained
12 ounces bacon, crisp-cooked and crumbled
$1/2$ cup chopped green onions
1 cup (4 ounces) grated Parmesan cheese
1 cup (4 ounces) shredded mozzarella cheese
$1/2$ cup (2 ounces) shredded Cheddar cheese

Combine the artichoke hearts, sour cream, mayonnaise, spinach, bacon, green onions, Parmesan cheese, mozzarella cheese and Cheddar cheese in a bowl and stir to mix. Spread in a 9×9-inch baking pan. Bake at 375 degrees for 30 minutes or until bubbly. Serve warm with flour tortillas or chips.

Yield: 6 cups

Shrimp Dip

8 ounces cream cheese, softened
$1/4$ cup mayonnaise
2 tablespoons finely chopped onion
2 tablespoons ketchup
$1/2$ teaspoon each paprika, cayenne pepper, and
  black pepper
4 ounces cooked shrimp, peeled, deveined and chopped
1 teaspoon finely chopped parsley

Beat the cream cheese and mayonnaise in a mixing bowl until fluffy. Stir in the onion, ketchup, paprika, cayenne pepper and black pepper. Fold in the shrimp. Spoon into a serving dish. Cover and chill thoroughly. Top with the parsley and serve with toast points or crackers.

Yield: 2 cups

Photograph for this recipe appears on page 8.

Columbus, Mississippi, also known as "The Friendly City," is a charming city of approximately 30,000 people located in northeastern Mississippi. Also the home of Columbus Air Force Base, Columbus is perhaps best known for its many fine antebellum homes and its annual pilgrimage held each April. During pilgrimage time, visitors flock to the city to tour the lovely houses and gardens and experience the hospitality of Columbus.

Welsh Rarebit

From Industrial Institute & College, II&C

1 tablespoon butter
1 tablespoon all-purpose flour
1/2 cup very hot milk or cream
8 ounces sharp Cheddar cheese, shredded
1/2 teaspoon salt
White or cayenne pepper to taste
1 loaf French bread, sliced and toasted

Melt the butter in a saucepan. Stir in the flour and cook briefly. Whisk in the hot milk gradually. Cook until slightly thickened, stirring constantly. Add the cheese and salt and season with pepper. Cook until the cheese is melted and the sauce is smooth, stirring constantly. Pour over the toasted bread or cut the bread into large cubes and dip in the cheese sauce as with a fondue.

Yield: 1 cup

Pimento Cheese Spread

40 ounces extra-sharp Cheddar cheese, shredded
1 (8-ounce) jar pimentos, chopped
2 cups mayonnaise
1/2 red bell pepper, finely chopped
2 tablespoons lemon juice
1 teaspoon prepared mustard
1 teaspoon Worcestershire sauce
1/2 teaspoon cayenne pepper
3 garlic cloves, minced

Combine the cheese, pimentos, mayonnaise, bell pepper, lemon juice, mustard, Worcestershire sauce, cayenne pepper and garlic in a large bowl. Stir to mix well. Cover and chill; the spread will thicken when it is thoroughly chilled. Use as a sandwich spread or to fill celery sticks or cherry tomatoes.

Yield: 4 pounds

"As for training young ladies through a long intellectual course, as we do young men, it can never be done. They will die in the process."

The opinion of a nineteenth-century gentleman, as quoted in Loyal Daughters *by* **Bridget Smith Pieschel** *and* **Stephen Robert Pieschel**

Ham and Cheese Balls

16 ounces cream cheese, softened
8 ounces sharp Cheddar cheese, shredded
1/2 onion, finely chopped
2 teaspoons Worcestershire sauce
1 teaspoon each lemon juice and prepared mustard
1/2 teaspoon each paprika and salt
2 1/2 ounces finely chopped ham
2 tablespoons each chopped parsley and chopped pimentos
3/4 cup walnuts or pecans, chopped
Paprika

Combine the cream cheese, Cheddar cheese, onion, Worcestershire sauce, lemon juice, mustard, paprika, salt, ham, parsley and pimentos in a large bowl and mix well. Cover and chill until almost firm. Shape into 2 balls and roll in the chopped walnuts. Cover with plastic wrap and chill overnight. Arrange on serving plates and sprinkle with additional paprika. Serve with assorted crackers.

Yield: 2 (1-pound) balls

Coleman's Favorite Cheese Logs

16 ounces sharp Cheddar cheese, shredded
16 ounces cream cheese, softened
8 ounces Roquefort cheese, crumbled
1 pound bacon, crisp-cooked and crumbled
1 small onion, grated
2 garlic cloves, minced
Worcestershire sauce to taste

Combine the Cheddar cheese, cream cheese, Roquefort cheese, bacon, onion and garlic in a large bowl. Season with Worcestershire sauce. Stir to mix well. Shape into 4 logs and cover each with plastic wrap. Chill until firm. Serve with crackers.

Yield: 4 (1-pound) logs

A Southerner can throw an entire party around a block of cream cheese and whatever is in the cupboard!

Cream Cheese Toppers

Top 1 (8-ounce) block of cream cheese with:

- *1 bottle "pickapeppa" sauce*
- *1 jar pepper jelly*
- *1/2 jar cocktail sauce and 1 (4-ounce) can crab or shrimp*
- *1 cup chunky salsa*

Serve any of the above with crackers or chips.

A selection of fine cheeses can be served in lieu of appetizers or hors d'oeuvre at most any party. The trick is to provide a good variety of cheeses along with the proper accompaniments. Start with a mild, soft cheese, such as a log of fresh chèvre (goat cheese). Then add a semi-soft, bloomy-rind cheese, such as Brie or Camembert. A wedge of hard, pressed cheese such as a true English Cheddar, Asiago, Emmentaler, or Edam can round out the selection. For more variety, include a washed-rind cheese (Oka, Taleggio, and Chaumes are popular) and a blue-veined cheese such as Roquefort or Stilton. In addition to crusty bread and mild crackers, offer your guests the proper condiments—cornichons (tiny sour pickles), quince or guava paste, honey (delicious with blue cheeses), and almonds, dates, or walnut halves. Everything can be purchased in advance and arranged on platters.

Baked Brie with Caramelized Pecans

3 tablespoons unsalted butter
1/4 cup packed dark brown sugar
1/4 cup pecans, chopped
1 sheet puff pastry, thawed
1 (4-inch) wheel Brie cheese (about 8 ounces)
1 egg white, lightly beaten

Melt the butter in a medium skillet over medium-high heat. Stir in the brown sugar and cook until the sugar dissolves. Stir in the pecans. Reduce the heat to low and cook for 5 minutes. Remove the pecan mixture and set aside to cool.

Unfold the puff pastry on a work surface. Mound the cooled pecan mixture in a circle in the center of the pastry. Place the Brie on top of the pecans. Bring the edges of the pastry together over the Brie and cut away any excess dough. Seal the edges with water.

Invert the wrapped Brie onto a parchment-lined baking sheet. Decorate the surface with the excess puff pastry pieces, if desired. Freeze for 1 hour.

Brush the dough with the egg white. Bake at 400 degrees for 30 minutes or until golden brown.

Yield: 4 servings

Yellow Birds

1 cup crème de banana liqueur
1 cup light rum
1/2 cup unsweetened pineapple juice
1/2 cup orange juice
1/4 cup lemon juice

Stir the banana liqueur, rum, pineapple juice, orange juice and lemon juice in a large pitcher; chill thoroughly. Serve over crushed ice in punch or julep cups.

Yield: 6 servings

Photograph for this recipe appears on page 8.

Lockheart Punch

1 1/2 gallons pineapple sherbet, preferably with fruit pieces
1 envelope unsweetened strawberry or fruit punch
   drink mix
2 liters lemon-lime soda or ginger ale

Place the sherbet in a punch bowl. Sprinkle the drink mix over the sherbet. Pour the lemon-lime soda over the sherbet. Let stand for 10 minutes or until the sherbet begins to melt; stir gently. Add 1 cup rum when the club advisor isn't looking.

Yield: 3 quarts

"On October 22 (1885) the happy and optimistic pioneering class assembled to begin proving its worth to the first state willing to pay for the education of its daughters."

Bridget Smith Pieschel and **Stephen Robert Pieschel** in Loyal Daughters

Ginger Lemonade

5 lemons
8 cups water
2¹/4 cups sugar
1 ounce fresh gingerroot, peeled and chopped

Juice the lemons and strain the juice. Set aside the lemon halves. Bring the water to a boil in a saucepan. Add the lemon halves, lemon juice, sugar and gingerroot. Reduce the heat to low and simmer gently for 10 minutes. Strain into a 4-quart heatproof pitcher. Add enough ice and cold water to fill the pitcher.

Yield: 4 quarts

Mint Tea

4 cups boiling water
2 large tea bags
¹/4 cup white grape juice
¹/4 cup lemon juice
¹/4 cup pineapple juice
4 sprigs of fresh mint

Pour the boiling water over the tea bags in a large heatproof pitcher. Let steep for 6 to 9 minutes. Remove the tea bags and discard. Stir in the white grape juice, lemon juice, pineapple juice and mint. Chill for 1 hour. Discard the mint. Pour over ice in glasses and garnish with additional mint.

Yield: 4 servings

"There I landed in a world to itself, and indeed it was all new to me. It was surging with twelve hundred girls. They came from every nook and corner of the state, from the Delta, the piney woods, the Gulf Coast, the black prairie, the red clay hills, and Jackson—as the capital city and only sizeable town, a region to itself."

Eudora Welty
on arriving as a student at Mississippi State College for Women in 1925, as told in One Writer's Beginnings

Banana Slush Punch

6 cups water
4 cups sugar
1 (46-ounce) can pineapple juice
1 (12-ounce) can frozen orange juice concentrate,
   reconstituted
1 (6-ounce) can frozen lemonade concentrate
5 bananas, mashed
12 liters lemon-lime soda or ginger ale

Combine the water and sugar in a large saucepan. Heat until the sugar dissolves, stirring occasionally. Remove from the heat and let cool. Stir in the pineapple juice, reconstituted orange juice concentrate, lemonade concentrate and bananas. Freeze until firm.

Remove from the freezer and let stand at room temperature for 1 hour or until softened. Scoop 1/3 of this mixture into a punch bowl and pour 4 liters of the lemon-lime soda over the top. Add a splash of rum if being served off campus! Return the remaining banana slush to the freezer. Replenish the punch bowl with more banana slush and lemon-lime soda as needed.

Yield: 50 servings

Orange Supreme Slush

1 cup water
1 cup sugar
1 cup milk
1 (6-ounce) can frozen orange juice concentrate
20 ice cubes

Combine the water, sugar, milk, orange juice concentrate and ice cubes in a blender and process until smooth. Add more ice if a thicker slush is desired.

Yield: 4 servings

Variation:
Add 1/2 cup fresh strawberries or pineapple chunks if desired.

The mothers of two of Mississippi's most famous writers attended The W. Maud Butler of Lafayette County was sent home for good after accumulating too many demerits at the school, but she recovered sufficiently from this unfortunate setback to marry Murry C. Falkner (spelling of the surname was changed later) and become the mother of William Faulkner. Edwina Dakin married Cornelius C. Williams and became the much-maligned mother of playwright Tennessee Williams.

Sangria

2/3 cup Sangria Base (below)
2 large oranges, sliced
2 lemons, sliced
1 (750-milliliter) bottle Spanish red wine
1/4 cup carbonated water

Combine the Sangria Base, oranges, lemons, wine and carbonated water in a large pitcher. Chill for at least 1 hour before serving.

Yield: 5 to 6 servings

Sangria Base

2 cups sugar
2 cups water
2 limes, sliced
2 large oranges, sliced
3 lemons, sliced

Combine the sugar, water, limes, oranges and lemons in a saucepan. Bring to a slow boil and simmer for 20 minutes. Remove from the heat and chill thoroughly. Strain and discard the fruit.

Yield: 3 cups

Mrs. Egger's Hot Fruit Punch

6 lemons
4 cups orange juice
2 cups pineapple juice
3 cups water
2 cinnamon sticks
1 to 2 cups sugar (or to taste)

Cut decorative pieces of zest from 3 of the lemons and set aside. Juice all of the lemons and strain out any seeds. Combine the lemon juice, orange juice, pineapple juice, water, cinnamon sticks and sugar in a large nonreactive saucepan. Add the pieces of lemon zest. Heat until the sugar dissolves and the punch is hot, stirring occasionally. Discard the cinnamon sticks.

Yield: 12 to 15 servings

Percolator Punch

8 cups cranberry juice cocktail
12 cups apple juice
2 cups pineapple juice
2/3 cup packed brown sugar
1/2 to 1 teaspoon salt
5 cinnamon sticks
2 teaspoons whole cloves

Pour the cranberry juice cocktail, apple juice and pineapple juice into the base of a 1 1/2-gallon coffee percolator. Place the brown sugar, salt, cinnamon sticks and cloves in the clean basket and set in the percolator. Run through a standard cycle and serve hot.

Yield: 25 to 30 cups

"Home is where you hang your childhood and Mississippi to me is the beauty spot of creation, a dark, wide, spacious land that you can breathe in."

Tennessee Williams, *whose birthplace was Columbus, Mississippi, as quoted in* Mississippi Home-Places: Notes on Literature and History *by Elmo Howell*

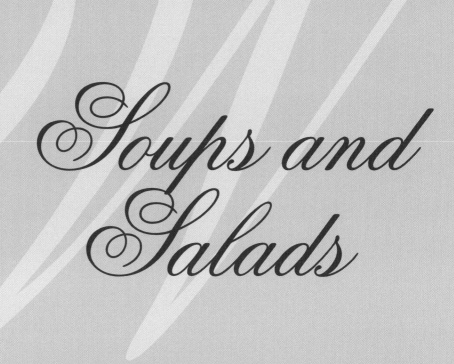

Soups and Salads

The Ginkgo Tree

For the last 103 autumns, the leaves of the ginkgo tree on front campus have turned gold in what seems to be a magical overnight occurrence. Just as unexpectedly, the leaves simultaneously drop from the tree to blanket the ground with a solid gold cover.

The W's ginkgo trees were planted in 1900 as part of an experiment by the Department of Agriculture to determine if the tree could survive a Southern climate. It has not only survived but has become part of one of the most treasured "W" traditions. The story has been told that if a leaf from the ginkgo tree at The W should fall on a "W" student at the same time a leaf from another ginkgo tree at Mississippi State University falls on a boy, the two are destined to meet and marry. Perhaps because a ginkgo tree is either male or female, or because the veins in the leaves continuously divide into two's, or maybe just because the tree is so beautiful, it seems the perfect setting for college romance.

Ginkgo trees are thought to be biologically the oldest trees in the world, dating back to 165 million years ago in China. Ginkgo trees exist in China today that are estimated to be as many as 3,000 years old. The trees adapted to Ice Age conditions and continue to thrive in modern cities, making the ginkgo tree a perfect symbol for the resiliency and strength of Mississippi University for Women.

Roasted Butternut Squash and Apple Soup

1 medium butternut squash, peeled, seeded and
    cut into wedges
2 tablespoons butter, melted
$1^1/_2$ teaspoons honey
4 Granny Smith apples, peeled, cored and sliced
2 tablespoons butter, melted
2 tablespoons cinnamon
$1/_2$ cup (1 stick) butter
$1/_3$ cup chopped onion
$1/_3$ cup chopped celery
4 cups chicken broth
1 cinnamon stick
Salt and white pepper to taste
3 tablespoons (or less) cinnamon
1 cup heavy cream

Arrange the squash on a parchment-lined baking sheet. Brush the squash with 2 tablespoons melted butter and drizzle with the honey. Bake at 350 degrees for 20 minutes or until fork-tender. Arrange the apples on a parchment-lined baking sheet. Brush the apples with 2 tablespoons melted butter and sprinkle with 2 tablespoons cinnamon. Bake at 350 degrees for 12 minutes or until fork-tender.

Melt $1/_2$ cup butter in a large saucepan over low heat. Add the onion and celery and sauté until translucent. Add the roasted squash, roasted apples, chicken broth and cinnamon stick. Bring to a simmer and cook for 10 minutes. Remove from the heat and discard the cinnamon stick. Process in batches in a food processor or blender until puréed. Strain through a mesh strainer back into the saucepan. Season with salt, white pepper and up to 3 tablespoons cinnamon. Stir in the cream and cook just until heated through. Ladle into hollowed-out small pumpkins or apple gourds. Garnish with a swirl of crème fraîche or sour cream.

Yield: 6 servings

Cream of Artichoke Soup

1/4 cup (1/2 stick) butter
3 tablespoons finely chopped onion
1 cup (about 2 ounces) thinly sliced fresh mushrooms
3 tablespoons all-purpose flour
1 cup chicken broth
1 1/2 cups half-and-half
1 cup milk
2 (14-ounce) cans artichoke hearts, drained well and
     chopped
1/2 teaspoon salt
Cayenne pepper to taste

Melt the butter in a saucepan over low heat. Add the onion and mushrooms. Cook for 5 minutes or until very tender. Stir in the flour and cook for 2 minutes. Whisk in the chicken broth gradually. Whisk in the half-and-half and milk. Cook over low heat until thickened. Stir in the artichoke hearts and salt and season with cayenne pepper. Cook until heated through. Ladle into bowls and garnish with chopped parsley.

Yield: 4 servings

Broccoli Cheese Soup

1 tablespoon butter
3/4 cup chopped onion
6 cups chicken broth
1 tablespoon salt
8 ounces egg noodles
1 pound broccoli, finely chopped
1/4 teaspoon garlic powder
14 ounces Cheddar cheese, shredded
6 cups milk
White pepper to taste

Melt the butter in a large saucepan. Add the onion and sauté until tender. Add the chicken broth and bring to a boil. Add the salt and noodles. Cook for 3 minutes. Stir in the broccoli and garlic powder. Cook for 4 minutes. Reduce the heat and add the cheese and milk. Simmer until the cheese melts. Season with white pepper.

Yield: 12 to 16 servings

Note:
Leftovers may be frozen.

Turnip Green Soup

1 pound country ham, cubed
2 cups chicken broth
2 medium red potatoes, cubed
1 large onion, chopped
1/2 cup sliced carrots
1/2 cup chopped celery
2 (15-ounce) cans navy beans
2 (10-ounce) packages frozen chopped turnip greens
1 tablespoon sugar
1 teaspoon pepper
Salt to taste
Garlic powder to taste

Place the ham, chicken broth, potatoes, onion, carrots and celery in a large saucepan. Bring to a boil and reduce the heat. Simmer for 10 minutes. Stir in the navy beans, turnip greens, sugar and pepper. Season with salt and garlic powder. Bring to a boil and reduce the heat. Simmer for 1 hour.

Yield: 10 servings

"One of the most fun things about The W was the singing. We sang in the dining hall. We had dormitory song competitions where we wrote parodies to popular hits. We sang at morning watch, noonday, and vespers at the Baptist Student Union. Being from the Coast, I did not get to go home often, especially with Saturday classes to attend. Therefore, we sang with gusto in December before leaving for the Christmas holidays:

Ten more days to vacation,
We will go to the station,
Back to civilization,
The train will carry us there.

Back to father and mother,
Back to sister and brother,
Back to kisses that smother,
The train will carry us there!"

Judge Mary Libby Bickerstaff Payne (Retired)
Class of 1954

Hot and Spicy Black Bean Chili

2 tablespoons olive oil or vegetable oil
1 large onion, chopped
2 large red or yellow bell peppers, chopped
4 garlic cloves, minced
4 (15-ounce) cans black beans, drained and rinsed
2 (14-ounce) cans diced tomatoes
3 jalapeño chiles, seeded and finely chopped
1 tablespoon chili powder
1 teaspoon dried oregano
$1^1/_2$ teaspoons cumin
$^1/_2$ teaspoon pepper
$^1/_4$ teaspoon salt
1 (11-ounce) can whole kernel corn, drained

Heat the olive oil in a Dutch oven or large saucepan over medium heat. Add the onion, bell peppers and garlic. Sauté for 8 minutes or until softened. Stir in the black beans, undrained tomatoes, jalapeño chiles, chili powder, oregano, cumin, pepper and salt. Bring to a boil and reduce the heat to low. Simmer, covered, for 30 minutes, stirring occasionally. Stir in the corn and cook for 5 minutes. Ladle into bowls and garnish with a dollop of sour cream or plain yogurt, shredded cheese and chopped fresh cilantro.

Yield: 12 to 16 servings

White Bean and Chicken Chili

2 tablespoons olive oil
2 tablespoons minced garlic
1 cup chopped onion
2 (15-ounce) cans (or more) chicken broth
4 (15-ounce) cans Great Northern beans, partially drained
4 cups chopped cooked chicken
2 teaspoons celery salt
2 teaspoons dried oregano
2 teaspoons cumin
1 teaspoon salt
White pepper to taste
1 (14-ounce) can diced tomatoes
2 (4-ounce) cans chopped green chiles

Heat the olive oil in a large saucepan. Add the garlic and onion and sauté until translucent but not brown. Stir in the chicken broth, beans, chicken, celery salt, oregano, cumin and salt. Season with white pepper. Cook until heated through. Purée the tomatoes and green chiles in a blender. Add to the saucepan. Bring to a boil and reduce the heat. Simmer for 3 hours. Add additional broth, if needed. Ladle into bowls and garnish with sour cream, crumbled queso blanco or chopped fresh cilantro.

Yield: 18 to 20 servings

Tuscan Bean Soup

8 ounces cannellini beans, soaked
2 tablespoons olive oil
1/2 teaspoon chili powder
1 large red onion, chopped
3 carrots, sliced
1 rib celery, chopped
1 bunch parsley, chopped
3 garlic cloves, minced
3/4 cup dry red wine
2 large tomatoes, peeled and chopped
2 cups chicken broth
4 ounces fresh spinach, rinsed and stems removed
Salt and pepper to taste
Italian bread, sliced and toasted
Olive oil
Fresh basil leaves, torn
Grated Parmesan cheese

Place the beans in a large saucepan and add enough cool water to cover. Bring to a boil and cook for 30 minutes. Drain and discard the cooking liquid. Mash 1/3 of the beans in a bowl with a fork.

Heat 2 tablespoons olive oil and the chili powder in a large saucepan over medium heat. Add the onion, carrots, celery and parsley. Sauté until the carrots are tender. Add the garlic and sauté for 2 minutes. Increase the heat and add the wine. Cook until most of the liquid evaporates. Reduce the heat. Add the mashed beans, remaining beans, tomatoes and chicken broth to the saucepan. Simmer for 45 minutes. Spread the spinach on top of the soup. Cover the pan and simmer for 5 minutes. Stir the soup and season with salt and pepper. Ladle into heated bowls. Top each with a slice of toasted bread, a drizzle of olive oil, torn basil leaves and a sprinkle of Parmesan cheese.

Yield: 4 to 6 servings

Note:
You may substitute 1 (14-ounce) can cannellini beans, well drained, for the uncooked beans. Do not cook for 30 minutes before adding to the soup.

Photograph for this recipe appears on page 28.

"You can take the girl away from The W, but you can't take The W out of her heart.

Sometimes living in Nashville makes me think like a country music lover, but I can truly say that I still have a special place in my heart for MUW. I have a deep desire for young people to find what I was privileged to experience at The W: cherished friends, caring professors, and the encouragement to contribute to the future in some way by using the unique gifts God gave to each one of us. I enjoy being part of helping MUW continue this tradition."

Andrea Godwin Overby
Class of 1968

Ham and Bean Soup

1 pound dried Great Northern beans
1 1/2 pounds cooked ham, cubed
6 cups water
1 teaspoon dried thyme leaves
1/2 teaspoon dried parsley flakes
1/2 teaspoon pepper
3 garlic cloves, minced
1 bay leaf
2 cups water
4 medium potatoes, peeled and coarsely chopped
3 carrots, sliced
1 medium onion, finely chopped
2 teaspoons salt

Rinse the beans and place in a large saucepan. Cover with water and let soak overnight. Drain and discard the water. Add the ham, 6 cups water, thyme, parsley flakes, pepper, garlic and bay leaf. Bring to a boil and reduce the heat. Simmer, covered, for 1 1/2 hours. Stir in 2 cups water, the potatoes, carrots, onion and salt. Simmer, covered, for 30 minutes or until the vegetables are tender. Remove the bay leaf and serve.

Yield: 10 to 12 servings

Beefy Vegetable Soup

1 pound ground beef
1 large onion, chopped
2 garlic cloves, minced
6 tablespoons tomato paste
2 cups beef broth
2 cups water
8 ounces mushrooms, sliced
1 cup chopped celery
6 large tomatoes, peeled and chopped
2 jalapeño chiles, finely chopped (optional)
6 large carrots, sliced
3 large potatoes, peeled and chopped
3/4 cup green peas
3/4 cup lima beans
1 teaspoon salt
1/2 teaspoon pepper

Brown the ground beef in a skillet with the onion and garlic, stirring until the ground beef is crumbly; drain. Place the ground beef mixture in a large saucepan. Stir in the tomato paste, beef broth, water, mushrooms, celery, tomatoes, jalapeño chiles, carrots and potatoes. Bring to a boil and reduce the heat. Simmer for 20 minutes. Stir in the peas, lima beans, salt and pepper. Simmer for 10 minutes.

Yield: 10 to 12 servings

Quick and Easy Santa Fe Soup

1¹/₂ to 2 pounds extra-lean ground beef or ground turkey
1 large onion, chopped
2 envelopes taco seasoning mix
2 envelopes ranch salad dressing mix
2 cups water
1 (15-ounce) can ranch-style pinto beans
1 (15-ounce) can red beans
1 (15-ounce) can black beans
1 (15-ounce) can kidney beans
1 (11-ounce) can whole kernel corn
1 (11-ounce) can white Shoe Peg corn
1 (14-ounce) can diced tomatoes
1 (14-ounce) can diced tomatoes with green chiles

Brown the ground beef with the onion in a Dutch oven or large saucepan, stirring until the ground beef is crumbly; drain. Stir in the taco seasoning mix, salad dressing mix, water, pinto beans, red beans, black beans, kidney beans, whole kernel corn, Shoe Peg corn, diced tomatoes and diced tomatoes with green chiles. Bring to a boil and reduce the heat. Simmer for 1¹/₂ to 2 hours. Serve in bread bowls if desired and garnish with sour cream, shredded cheese and chopped fresh cilantro.

Yield: 12 to 16 servings

Chicken Noodle Soup

4 boneless skinless chicken breasts
4 cups chicken broth
2 tablespoons olive oil
1 rib celery, chopped
2 pounds carrots, chopped
1^1/$_2$ cups uncooked egg noodles
^{1}/$_2$ teaspoon salt
^{1}/$_2$ teaspoon pepper

Combine the chicken breasts and chicken broth in a saucepan. Simmer until the chicken is firm and cooked through. Remove the chicken; shred when cool. Set aside the broth.

Heat the olive oil in a large saucepan. Add the celery and carrots and sauté until the vegetables are tender. Add the reserved broth, noodles, salt and pepper. Simmer until the noodles are cooked. Stir in the shredded chicken.

Yield: 4 to 6 servings

"A girl has the right to demand such training that she can win her own way to independence, thereby making marriage not a necessity, but a choice."

President William Howard Taft,
from his address to II&C in Columbus, Mississippi, October 12, 1910

Crab and Asparagus Soup

4 cups chicken broth
1 teaspoon finely chopped peeled fresh gingerroot
8 ounces asparagus spears, cut diagonally into 1-inch pieces
1 egg, well beaten
1 tablespoon cornstarch
2 tablespoons water
2 teaspoons dry sherry
1 teaspoon Asian sesame oil
1 teaspoon soy sauce
1 cup cooked lump crab meat, flaked
Salt and white pepper to taste

Combine the chicken broth and gingerroot in a large saucepan. Bring to a rolling boil over medium-high heat. Add the asparagus and reduce the heat to medium. Simmer, covered, for 3 minutes or until the asparagus is tender-crisp. Reduce the heat to medium-low.

Stir 2 tablespoons of the hot broth into the beaten egg in a small bowl. Pour the egg mixture slowly into the broth to form even threads of cooked egg, stirring constantly. Mix the cornstarch and water in a small bowl. Add the cornstarch mixture, sherry, sesame oil and soy sauce to the soup.

Cook for 1 minute or until slightly thickened, stirring constantly. Stir in the crab meat. Cook for 2 to 3 minutes or just until heated through. Season with salt and white pepper.

Yield: 4 to 6 servings

In 1885, students got only Christmas Day off from classes, and few could travel home for such a short duration. Columbus residents stepped in and elaborately decorated the dining hall for Christmas dinner. This tradition of decorating the dining hall continued, and Shattuck Dining Hall was decorated each Christmas with holiday centerpieces and a Christmas tree. The same star perched atop the tree for many years, causing one student to lament, "When I graduate, get a job, and get rich, I'm going to buy a new star!" "Over my dead body!" was the response. "That same star was on the tree when my mother came here!"

Gulf Coast Seafood Gumbo

6 tablespoons all-purpose flour
5 tablespoons bacon drippings
1 large onion, chopped
1 cup chopped celery
1 green bell pepper, finely chopped
1 (29-ounce) can tomatoes
1 (8-ounce) can tomato sauce
1 (10-ounce) package frozen sliced okra
5 to 6 cups water
1 teaspoon sugar
1 teaspoon salt
1 teaspoon pepper
1 bay leaf
1/2 teaspoon dried oregano
1/2 teaspoon dried basil
1/2 teaspoon cinnamon
1 cup dry white wine
1/2 teaspoon Worcestershire sauce
1 pound cooked shrimp, peeled and deveined
2 cups cooked crab meat, flaked
1 pint shucked oysters (optional)
1 to 2 tablespoons filé powder (optional)
Hot cooked white rice

43

A roux is used to thicken many sauces and soups. It is equal parts of fat and flour slowly cooked over low heat. It should be stirred constantly to prevent burning. There are three classic roux based on color—white, blond, and brown. A white roux is cooked just enough to remove the starchy taste and has the most thickening power but the least amount of flavor. Blond roux has a light golden color, and brown roux has a nutty color and flavor, but thickens the least. Brown roux is used for dark soups and sauces and is a key ingredient for making gumbo.

Combine the flour and bacon drippings in a Dutch oven or large saucepan. Cook over low heat to make a rich brown roux, stirring constantly to prevent burning. Add the onion, celery and bell pepper and sauté until the vegetables are softened. Stir in the tomatoes, tomato sauce, okra, water, sugar, salt, pepper, bay leaf, oregano, basil, cinnamon, wine and Worcestershire sauce. Cook over medium-low heat for 2 to 4 hours. Stir in the shrimp, crab meat, oysters and filé powder 1 hour before serving. Remove the bay leaf and serve over piping hot rice.

Yield: 12 to 16 servings

Note:
Filé powder will thicken the gumbo and should be used only if a thick gumbo is desired.

Carrot Soup

2 tablespoons butter
1 cup chopped onion
1 pound carrots, chopped
4 cups chicken broth
1 bay leaf
$1^1/_2$ teaspoons salt
$1/_8$ teaspoon white pepper
$1/_2$ cup fresh orange juice
1 cup half-and-half
1 tablespoon orange liqueur

Melt the butter in a large saucepan. Add the onion and carrots. Sauté until the onion is translucent but not brown. Stir in the chicken broth, bay leaf, salt and white pepper. Bring to a boil and reduce the heat. Simmer, covered, for 20 to 30 minutes or until the carrots are tender. Remove the bay leaf.

Purée the soup in a blender or with an immersion blender. Return the soup to the saucepan. Whisk in the orange juice, half-and-half and orange liqueur. Heat gently and serve immediately or chill for at least 6 hours and serve cold. Garnish with chopped chives.

Yield: 8 servings

Cucumber Avocado Bisque

1 medium cucumber, peeled and seeded
1 ripe avocado, peeled and pitted
3 green onions, chopped
1 cup chicken broth
1 cup sour cream
2 tablespoons fresh lemon juice
1/2 teaspoon salt
White pepper to taste

Combine the cucumber, avocado, green onions, chicken broth, sour cream, lemon juice and salt in a blender. Season with white pepper. Process at low speed for 10 to 15 seconds. Cover and chill thoroughly. Season with additional salt and white pepper, if desired. Pour into bowls and garnish with chopped parsley or a dollop of sour cream.

Yield: 4 servings

Ginger Pear Salad

2 ripe pears, peeled, cored and thinly sliced
1 cup red seedless grapes
1 head Boston lettuce, torn into bite-size pieces
6 tablespoons vegetable oil
2 tablespoons lime juice
1 teaspoon sugar
1/4 cup crystallized ginger, chopped
Salt and pepper to taste

Place the pears, grapes and lettuce in a serving bowl. Whisk the oil, lime juice, sugar and crystallized ginger in a bowl. Season with salt and pepper. Drizzle over the salad and toss gently. Serve immediately.

Yield: 6 servings

"Columbus is a place where Southern hospitality greets you when you come and makes you never want to leave. It's a place where the historic architecture of old Greek columns and cupolas maintains an important presence amidst marvelous modern structures. This beautiful blending not only occurs in the city's architecture but also in its people."

Paula Ramsey *and* **Jennifer Ramsey** *in* A Lady's Day Out in Mississippi

Bing Cherry Salad

1 (14-ounce) can dark Bing cherries, pitted
1 (8-ounce) can crushed pineapple
1 (4-ounce) package black cherry gelatin
1 cup cola
1/2 cup chopped pecans

Drain the cherries and pineapple, reserving the juices. Combine the reserved juices in a measuring cup, adding enough water to measure 1 cup. Pour into a saucepan. Bring to a boil. Combine the juice mixture and gelatin in a bowl and stir until the gelatin dissolves. Stir in the cola and drained fruit. Stir in the pecans. Pour into an oiled mold and chill, covered, for several hours or until set.

Yield: 6 to 8 servings

Southern Pickled Peaches

1 cup water
1 cup cider vinegar
2 cups sugar
2 cinnamon sticks
1 teaspoon mixed pickling spice
8 to 12 medium peaches, peeled, halved and pitted

Combine the water, vinegar, sugar, cinnamon sticks and pickling spice in a large saucepan. Bring to a boil. Add the peach halves and simmer for 10 minutes. Ladle the peaches into hot sterilized jars. Add the hot syrup, leaving 1/2 inch headspace; seal with 2-piece lids. Process in a boiling water bath for 20 minutes.

Yield: 1 to 2 quarts

Note:
You may store the pickled peaches in the refrigerator if you don't wish to can them.

Mandarin Orange and Romaine Salad

1/4 cup white wine
1 tablespoon sugar
1/2 cup vegetable oil
Dash of Tabasco sauce
Salt and pepper to taste
3/4 cup slivered almonds
3 tablespoons sugar
1/2 cup mandarin orange sections
1/2 cup sliced scallions
1/2 cup chopped celery
1 head romaine lettuce, chopped

Whisk the wine, 1 tablespoon sugar, oil and Tabasco sauce in a bowl. Season with salt and pepper.

Combine the almonds and 3 tablespoons sugar in a skillet. Cook over medium heat until the sugar coats the almonds, stirring frequently. Remove to waxed paper to cool. Break into pieces when cool.

Combine the mandarin orange sections, scallions, celery and romaine in a large bowl. Add the dressing and toss to coat. Top with the sugared almonds.

Yield: 4 servings

Ralph's Crunchy Strawberry Salad

1 (3-ounce) package ramen noodles
2 tablespoons butter
2 heads Bibb lettuce
1 pint strawberries, sliced
1 cup toasted pecans, chopped
Raspberry Orange Vinaigrette (below)

Crumble the noodles. Discard the seasoning packet or reserve for another use. Melt the butter in a skillet. Add the crumbled noodles and sauté until golden brown. Remove the noodles and let cool. Arrange the lettuce and strawberries on plates. Top with the cooled noodles and pecans. Drizzle with Raspberry Orange Vinaigrette.

Yield: 8 servings

Raspberry Orange Vinaigrette

1 1/2 cups orange juice
1/3 cup raspberry jam
1/4 cup olive oil
1/4 cup balsamic vinegar
1/2 teaspoon five-spice powder
1/8 teaspoon allspice

Whisk the orange juice, raspberry jam, olive oil, vinegar, five-spice powder and allspice in a bowl. Cover and chill overnight to allow the flavors to blend.

Yield: 2 1/3 cups

Broccoli Salad

1 bunch broccoli, cut into florets
1/3 cup raisins
2 green onions, finely sliced
8 ounces bacon, crisp-cooked and crumbled
1 (8-ounce) can sliced water chestnuts, drained
1/2 to 1 cup mayonnaise
1/4 to 1/2 cup sugar
1 tablespoon vinegar

Combine the broccoli, raisins, green onions, bacon and water chestnuts in a bowl. Toss to mix. Stir the mayonnaise, sugar and vinegar in a bowl until the sugar dissolves. Add to the broccoli mixture and toss to coat.

Yield: 6 to 8 servings

The West's Best Slaw

1 large head cabbage, shredded
1 large bell pepper, chopped
1 large red onion, sliced into thin rings
1 cup cider vinegar
1/2 cup vegetable oil
1/2 cup sugar
Salt and pepper to taste

Mix the cabbage, bell pepper and onion in a large bowl. Combine the vinegar, oil and sugar in a saucepan. Heat until the sugar dissolves, stirring frequently. Pour over the vegetables and toss to coat. Season with salt and pepper. Cover and chill overnight.

Yield: 10 to 12 servings

The cookbook committee probably received more variations of this Broccoli Salad recipe than any other. Literally dozens of people submitted their take on the popular raw broccoli salad. Common variations included seedless grapes, sunflower seeds, slivered red onions, toasted almonds, celery, cauliflower florets, or shredded Cheddar cheese. Broccoli, bacon, some type of onion, and the mayonnaise-sugar-vinegar dressing seems to be the foundation for this salad. After that, your creativity is the only limit.

The standard formula for all vinaigrette dressings is three parts oil to one part vinegar. In other words, whisk 1 cup oil into 1/3 cup vinegar. With that foundation, you can add salt and pepper, herbs, mustard, garlic, nuts, chopped dried fruit, or other seasonings to suit your preference. As for the oil and vinegar—just be sure to use flavorful products that will complement each other. Try extra-virgin olive oil with balsamic vinegar; sherry wine vinegar with walnut oil or hazelnut oil; or tarragon vinegar with bland vegetable oil. For the best texture, add the seasonings to the vinegar, then whisk in the oil. If the dressing separates before use, simply whisk it back together just before serving.

Chinese Cabbage Salad with Sesame Ginger Dressing

$1/4$ cup sesame oil
$1/4$ cup vegetable oil
$1/2$ cup soy sauce
$3/4$ cup rice wine vinegar
$1/4$ cup packed brown sugar
$1/4$ cup chopped fresh gingerroot
$1/4$ cup fresh cilantro, chopped
2 garlic cloves, minced
1 shallot, minced
1 head napa cabbage, shredded
1 medium red bell pepper, julienned
6 ounces fresh mushrooms, thinly sliced
$1/2$ cup fresh bean sprouts
1 pint cherry tomatoes (optional)

Purée the sesame oil, vegetable oil, soy sauce, vinegar, brown sugar, gingerroot, cilantro, garlic and shallot in a blender.

Mix the cabbage, bell pepper, mushrooms, bean sprouts and cherry tomatoes in a large bowl. Add the dressing and toss gently to coat. Cover and chill.

Yield: 8 servings

Corn Bread Salad

3 medium tomatoes, peeled, seeded and chopped
1/2 cup sliced green onions
1/2 cup chopped bell pepper
1/2 cup chopped sweet pickles
10 slices bacon, crisp-cooked and crumbled
1 cup mayonnaise
1/2 cup sweet pickle juice
6 dry corn bread muffins, cut into small pieces

Combine the tomatoes, green onions, bell pepper, pickles, bacon, mayonnaise and pickle juice in a bowl. Stir to mix well. Alternate layers of the tomato mixture and corn bread in a baking dish. Cover and chill for at least 2 hours before serving.

Yield: 8 servings

Marinated Cucumbers

6 medium cucumbers
2 tablespoons salt
1 red onion, thinly sliced
3 cups white or cider vinegar
3 cups water
3 cups sugar
2 tablespoons salt
2 teaspoons pepper
2 teaspoons dried dill weed

Peel the cucumbers and slice 1/4 to 1/2 inch thick. Place them in a bowl and cover with water and ice. Add 2 tablespoons salt. Let stand for 10 minutes. Drain the cucumbers and place in a bowl with the onion. Whisk the vinegar, 3 cups water, sugar, 2 tablespoons salt, pepper and dill weed in a bowl. Pour over the cucumbers and onion. Cover and chill overnight.

Yield: 8 servings

Spinach and Tomato Salad

4 large tomatoes, peeled, seeded and chopped
2 garlic cloves, minced
$1/2$ teaspoon salt
$1/4$ teaspoon white pepper
Juice of 1 lime
8 ounces fresh spinach, rinsed and stems removed
1 small red onion, thinly sliced
2 tablespoons chopped pitted kalamata olives
6 ounces feta cheese, crumbled
2 tablespoons toasted pine nuts
2 tablespoons chopped pitted kalamata olives

Mix the tomatoes, garlic, salt, white pepper and lime juice in a bowl. Cover and chill overnight.

Toss the spinach, onion and 2 tablespoons olives in a bowl. Add the tomato mixture and toss to mix. Top with the feta cheese, pine nuts and 2 tablespoons olives.

Yield: 6 to 8 servings

Photograph for this recipe appears on page 28.

"In 1953, two of our home economic students did their student teaching in Macon. Their students were demonstrating their skills with a Parent's Brunch, and much effort had gone into the event. Guests complimented the food as they sipped their spiced tea in delicate china cups. Accolades were showered upon the students and their student teachers, and one by one the guests departed. As cleanup commenced, the student teachers discovered that instead of spiced tea, the parents had all been served water from wieners cooked earlier in the day. Gracious are those who sip wiener water and never even ask for sugar!"

Martha Jo Ballard Mims
Class of 1964
Faculty, 1967-2000

Tabouli

2 1/2 cups bulgur (cracked wheat)
1 tablespoon salt
2 teaspoons pepper
1 teaspoon allspice
1/2 teaspoon cinnamon
3 large tomatoes, chopped
2 bunches green onions, chopped
3 bunches parsley, stems removed and chopped
   (about 6 cups)
1 cup chopped fresh mint
1/2 cup olive oil
1 cup fresh lemon juice

Rinse the bulgur in cool water and place it in a large bowl.
Cover with cold water and let soak for 45 minutes. Drain the
water and squeeze as much liquid as possible from the bulgur.
Place the drained bulgur in a large bowl and add the salt, pepper,
allspice and cinnamon. Toss to mix. Add the tomatoes, green
onions, parsley and mint and toss to mix. Add the olive oil and
lemon juice and toss to mix well. Cover and chill for 3 hours
before serving.

   Yield: 12 to 16 servings

*International cuisine was
considered quite innovative
in 1956, when Ethel
Summerour (Class of 1926),
MSCW dietitian, created the
idea of international dinners
after a trip to Europe. Her
inaugural international
dinner was described on the
menu as "an introduction
to the delights of French
cooking." The dining hall
was decorated; the servers
wore white blouses, dark
skirts, red or blue ties, and
tiny aprons with big bows.
Placemats were shipped
from Pam Pam, Miss
Summerour's favorite
restaurant in France, and
the menu cover was copied
from a French cookbook
entitled* What's Cooking
in France.

Broccoli and Pasta Salad

1 (20-ounce) package cheese tortellini
3 ounces fettuccini noodles, broken into halves
2^1/2 cups cherry tomatoes, halved
2 cups broccoli florets
2 cups sliced fresh mushrooms
2 cups snow peas, blanched and drained
^{1}/2 cup chopped green onions
^{1}/4 cup (1 ounce) grated Parmesan cheese
^{1}/3 cup red wine vinegar
2 garlic cloves, minced
2 tablespoons chopped fresh parsley
2 teaspoons dried basil
^{1}/2 teaspoon dried dill weed
1 teaspoon salt
^{1}/2 teaspoon pepper
^{1}/2 teaspoon dried oregano
^{1}/2 teaspoon sugar
1^1/2 teaspoons Dijon mustard
^{1}/3 cup canola oil
^{1}/3 cup olive oil

Cook the tortellini and fettuccini in separate saucepans of rapidly boiling water until done. Drain, rinse with cold water and chill. Combine the cherry tomatoes, broccoli, mushrooms, snow peas, green onions and cheese in a large bowl. Cover and chill. Process the vinegar, garlic, parsley, basil, dill weed, salt, pepper, oregano, sugar and Dijon mustard in a food processor or blender. Add the canola oil and olive oil gradually, processing constantly until smooth.

Add the chilled cooked pasta to the vegetables and toss to mix. Add the dressing and toss well to coat. Chill thoroughly before serving.

Yield: 16 to 20 servings

Pasta and Pepper Salad

16 ounces rotini, cooked and drained
2 to 3 cups chopped fresh broccoli
1 1/2 cups mushrooms, sliced
1 cup red bell pepper, cut into strips
1 cup green bell pepper, cut into strips
1 cup yellow bell pepper, cut into strips
1 cup sliced black olives
3/4 cup mayonnaise
1/3 cup olive oil
1/3 cup cider vinegar
1/4 cup sugar
2 teaspoons salt
1 1/2 teaspoons pepper
1 teaspoon paprika

Combine the pasta, broccoli, mushrooms, red bell pepper, green bell pepper, yellow bell pepper and olives in a large bowl. Cover and chill.

Whisk the mayonnaise, olive oil, vinegar, sugar, salt, pepper and paprika in a bowl. Pour over the salad and toss gently to coat. Cover and chill for at least 3 hours. Make a day ahead for best results.

Yield: 12 to 16 servings

The hospitality of Maureen and Ed Watt and their Silver Platter Restaurant's delicious Magnolia Heritage Salad helped gain broad support for MUW from the members of the Mississippi Legislature.

"To prepare the salad, cut 2 pineapples lengthwise into halves. Scoop out the centers to form shells, reserving the pineapple. Mix 2 cups smoked turkey breast chunks, 1 cup coarsely chopped celery, 2 large bananas, thickly sliced, 1 large apple, cubed, 1 cup seedless grape halves and 1 cup canned pineapple chunks in a large bowl. Blend 1/2 cup mayonnaise, 1/2 cup sour cream, 3/4 cup muscadine preserves and 2 cups whipped cream in a small bowl. Stir into the turkey mixture. Spoon into the pineapple shells. Garnish with the reserved pineapple, toasted pecans, strawberries, kiwifruit and melon in season."

Maureen Tadlock Watt
Class of 1961

Asian Chicken and Pasta Salad

2 tablespoons vegetable oil
3 chicken breasts, thinly sliced
8 ounces uncooked rice noodles
1/2 cup slivered almonds, toasted
1/2 head cabbage, shredded
4 green onions, chopped
1 carrot, finely chopped
4 ounces snow peas
4 ounces water chestnuts, chopped
1/2 cup vegetable oil
1 1/2 teaspoons sesame oil
3 tablespoons rice wine vinegar
3 tablespoons soy sauce
2 tablespoons sugar
1 teaspoon salt
1 1/2 teaspoons pepper
1 tablespoon chopped fresh gingerroot
1 bunch (3 ounces) fresh cilantro, chopped

Heat the oil in a skillet. Add the chicken and sauté until cooked through. Remove to a plate and let cool. Boil the rice noodles in water to cover in a saucepan for 3 minutes. Plunge into cold water to stop the cooking process; drain. Let the noodles stand until cool. Cut into 2- to 3-inch pieces. Toss the chicken, noodles, almonds, cabbage, green onions, carrot, snow peas and water chestnuts together in a large bowl.

Whisk the vegetable oil, sesame oil, vinegar, soy sauce, sugar, salt, pepper, gingerroot and cilantro in a bowl. Pour over the salad and toss to coat.

Yield: 6 to 8 servings

Gourmet Chicken Salad

8 cups chopped or shredded cooked chicken breast
2 cups chopped celery
1 (20-ounce) can pineapple tidbits, drained
1 (8-ounce) can sliced water chestnuts, drained
2 pounds seedless grapes, halved
2 cups slivered almonds, toasted
2 1/2 cups mayonnaise
2 1/2 teaspoons curry powder
2 teaspoons soy sauce
Juice of 1 lemon
Salt, pepper and paprika to taste

Toss the chicken, celery, pineapple, water chestnuts, grapes and almonds together gently in a large bowl. Whisk the mayonnaise, curry powder, soy sauce and lemon juice in a bowl. Add to the salad and toss gently to mix. Season with salt, pepper and paprika. Chill before serving.

Yield: 18 servings

In October of each year MUW hosts its Welty Weekend, where well-known writers come to The W to discuss their work for the benefit and delight of students and the many alumni and other visitors who regard this occasion as a highlight of their year. One of the favorite events of the weekend is the Andrea Godwin Overby Journalism Forum, where a journalist of national stature lectures on current events and journalism in general. Speakers for Welty Weekend have included such nationally known authors as John Grisham, Fannie Flagg, and George Plimpton.

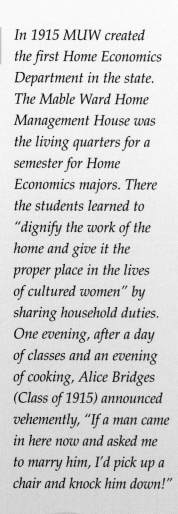

Lobster Salad

1 head romaine, cut crosswise into thin strips
1 pound cooked fresh lobster meat
1 cup finely chopped scallions
2 tablespoons chopped fresh basil
1 tablespoon Dijon mustard
1/4 cup white wine vinegar
2 tablespoons finely chopped shallots
1 hard-cooked egg, finely chopped
Salt and pepper to taste
1 cup canola oil

Place the romaine in a salad bowl and arrange the lobster on top. Sprinkle with the chopped scallions and basil. Whisk the Dijon mustard, vinegar, shallots and chopped egg in a bowl. Season with salt and pepper. Add the canola oil in a steady stream, whisking constantly. Drizzle the dressing over the salad or serve the dressing on the side.

Yield: 4 servings

Shrimp Salad

1 pound unpeeled medium shrimp
3 to 4 tablespoons mayonnaise
4^1/$_2$ teaspoons fresh lemon juice
1 tablespoon Italian salad dressing mix
^{1}/$_4$ teaspoon cayenne pepper
Salt to taste
^{3}/$_4$ cup finely chopped celery
2 tablespoons finely chopped onion
4 hard-cooked eggs, chopped
Lettuce

Cook the shrimp in boiling water in a saucepan for 4 minutes or until the shrimp turn pink. Drain and cool. Peel, devein and cut each shrimp into 2 or 3 pieces. Whisk the mayonnaise, lemon juice, salad dressing mix and cayenne pepper in a bowl. Season with salt. Add the shrimp, celery, onion and chopped eggs. Toss gently to mix. Cover and chill thoroughly. Serve on a bed of lettuce and garnish with slices of avocado.

Yield: 4 servings

Main Dishes

Dining Room at Puckett House

Shattuck Hall

Shattuck Hall and delicious food are synonymous to everyone who graduated from The W before 1974. The dining room offered the students family-style service that both nourished and trained the thousands of young women who took their places at the damask-covered tables from 1912 until 1970. Shattuck Hall opened in 1912 as the senior dormitory and dining hall. It was named by the students of the Classes of 1911 and 1912 for Melissa Curtis Shattuck (1841-1929), who served as the Director of Housekeeping at II&C for twenty-three years.

Shattuck Hall was partially destroyed by fire in 1953, and the four-story structure was renovated to become the two-story structure that stands today. The new dining hall was Mississippi's largest dining facility at the time.

Since the closing of Shattuck Dining Hall in 1970, all students have been served by the Nancy Hogarth Cafeteria. The tradition of exceptional cuisine returned to Shattuck Hall with the opening of the MUW Culinary Arts Institute in 1996. Once again, Shattuck Hall and delicious food are synonymous to all who know The W.

Beef Stroganoff

1 tablespoon butter
1¹/2 pounds well-trimmed beef tenderloin or
   round steak, cut into thin strips
1 tablespoon butter
1 large onion, chopped
8 ounces sliced fresh mushrooms
1 bay leaf
3/4 cup sherry or red wine
2 tablespoons cornstarch
1 (14-ounce) can beef broth
1/2 teaspoon salt
Pepper to taste
3/4 cup sour cream
1 tablespoon finely chopped fresh dill weed
20 ounces thick egg noodles, cooked

Melt 1 tablespoon butter in a skillet. Add the beef and sauté
briefly or to desired doneness. Remove the beef to a plate and
cover. Add 1 tablespoon butter, the onion and mushrooms to the
skillet. Sauté until the vegetables are tender and light brown. Add
the bay leaf and sherry. Cook until the liquid is reduced by half.
Remove the bay leaf and discard.

Mix the cornstarch and beef broth in a bowl. Stir into the
skillet. Bring to a boil and cook until thickened. Add the salt and
season with pepper. Add the cooked beef and any juices that
have collected on the plate. Cook until heated through, stirring
occasionally. Stir in the sour cream and dill weed. Heat thoroughly
but do not allow to boil. Serve over the hot cooked noodles.

Yield: 6 servings

"Good gravy is like a good black dress. It can hide a multitude of sins."

Fannie Flagg
Former Welty Weekend speaker

Steak with Port and Mushroom Sauce

1 teaspoon vegetable oil
2 (5- to 6-ounce) well-trimmed beef tenderloin steaks
Salt and pepper to taste
4 ounces portobello mushrooms, thinly sliced
1/2 cup port
2 tablespoons sour cream
1/2 teaspoon cornstarch

Heat a medium skillet over high heat. Add the oil when the skillet is very hot and then the steaks. Brown the steaks for 1 to 2 minutes per side or to desired doneness. Season lightly with salt and pepper. Remove the steaks to a plate; cover and keep warm.

Add the mushrooms to the skillet and sauté for 1 minute. Add the port and simmer for 1 minute or until the port is reduced slightly. Reduce the heat to low. Stir the sour cream and cornstarch in a small bowl. Add to the skillet and cook until smooth and thickened, stirring constantly. Do not allow to boil. Season with salt and pepper. Pour the mushroom sauce over the steaks and serve.

Yield: 2 servings

Apple Orchard Pot Roast

2 teaspoons vegetable oil
1 (3-pound) chuck roast
1 1/2 cups apple juice
1/2 cup orange juice
1 cup dry white wine
6 garlic cloves, chopped
1/2 teaspoon salt
6 whole cloves
1 cinnamon stick
3 carrots, sliced
2 sweet potatoes, peeled and quartered

Heat the oil in a Dutch oven over medium-high heat. Add the roast and brown on all sides. Add the apple juice, orange juice, wine, garlic, salt, cloves and cinnamon stick. Bring to a boil. Reduce the heat and simmer for 10 minutes. Remove from the heat and cover.

Bake at 300 degrees for 1 hour. Turn the roast over and add the carrots and sweet potatoes. Increase the oven temperature to 350 degrees and bake, covered, for 2 hours. Uncover during the last 20 minutes of cooking. Remove the roast to a cutting board and let stand for 10 minutes before carving. Serve with the vegetables.

Yield: 6 servings

"I lived in 'The Mag' during my first three years at MUW. While its former splendor was fading (the pink beauty parlor had long been closed), it still seemed very luxurious to me. It had its own cafeteria on the first floor, a sunny room that opened on to a patio leading to a shamrock-shaped pool. My favorite lunchtime dish was beef stroganoff with mushrooms and egg noodles. Often we'd sit enjoying a plateful of that stroganoff while just outside we could see other girls basting themselves in baby oil, broiled to a turn. Inside and out, everything was cooked to perfection!"

Bridget Smith Pieschel, Ph.D.
*Head of Division of Humanities, MUW
Class of 1979*

Beef Teriyaki

1/4 cup soy sauce
2 tablespoons dry sherry
1 tablespoon brown sugar
2 garlic cloves, minced
1 teaspoon ground ginger, or
    2 teaspoons finely chopped fresh gingerroot
12 ounces beef flank steak, cut into 1/2-inch strips
1 tablespoon vegetable oil
2 large carrots, chopped
3/4 cup snow peas
3/4 cup broccoli florets
41/2 teaspoons cornstarch
11/2 cups beef broth
Salt and pepper to taste
3 cups hot cooked rice

Mix the soy sauce, sherry, brown sugar, garlic and ginger in a bowl. Add the beef and marinate for 10 minutes. Remove the beef and discard the marinade. Heat the oil in a skillet. Stir-fry the beef in the hot oil until brown.

Add the carrots, snow peas and broccoli and stir-fry until tender-crisp. Mix the cornstarch and beef broth in a bowl. Stir into the skillet. Bring to a boil and cook for 1 minute. Season with salt and pepper. Serve over the hot rice.

Yield: 4 servings

"Family-style meal service prevailed at The W from 1885 until 1970. Students were served on crisply-laundered damask tablecloths and napkins with senior or faculty hostesses at each table. Students waited outside the dining room doors until a whistle announced the beginning of each meal. Friends appointed their most aggressive cohort to rush in to claim their table. Dignity was a casualty of the system as one enthusiastic student sprinted across the freshly-waxed floors of the dining hall and slid to her desired table which she had to claim from beneath the damask tablecloth."

Ricki Rayner Garrett
Class of 1973

Beef-Stuffed Zucchini

4 medium zucchini
12 ounces ground chuck
$1/4$ cup bread crumbs
$1/4$ cup (1 ounce) grated Parmesan cheese
$1/4$ cup tomato juice
2 eggs, beaten
2 tablespoons finely chopped fresh parsley
$1/2$ teaspoon crushed dried rosemary
$1/4$ teaspoon garlic salt
$1/8$ teaspoon pepper

Cook the whole zucchini in a large saucepan of boiling water for 7 minutes or until tender but still firm. Drain and let cool until cool enough to handle. Cut each zucchini in half lengthwise. Remove the pulp, leaving a $1/4$-inch-thick shell. Chop the pulp and set aside.

Brown the ground chuck in a large skillet, stirring until crumbly; drain. Pat with paper towels to remove as much fat as possible. Combine the cooked ground chuck, zucchini pulp, bread crumbs, cheese, tomato juice, eggs, parsley, rosemary, garlic salt and pepper in a bowl. Stir to mix. Fill the zucchini shells with the ground chuck mixture. Place in a greased baking dish and bake at 350 degrees for 25 to 30 minutes.

Yield: 4 servings

Gus' Sugar-Glazed Barbecue Sauce for Ribs

President William Howard Taft visited The W in 1910, and a gala barbecue was held on campus in his honor. Students in blue uniforms with embroidered white organdy aprons served the honored guests. The chair in which President Taft was seated broke from the strain of the barbecue-filled President, but a replacement was quickly provided with few ever knowing of the mishap...until now.

1/2 teaspoon coriander seeds
2 teaspoons mustard seeds
1/2 teaspoon black peppercorns
3 tablespoons kosher salt
1/4 cup sugar
1 tablespoon granulated garlic
1/2 teaspoon ground cumin
1/2 teaspoon ground cloves
1/4 teaspoon ground nutmeg
1/2 teaspoon chili powder
1/4 teaspoon cayenne pepper
1 teaspoon crushed red pepper
1/2 cup vegetable oil
1/4 cup molasses

Place the coriander seeds, mustard seeds and peppercorns in a small skillet. Toast over medium-high heat until they become fragrant and popping or sizzling sounds are heard. Remove from the heat immediately. Grind the toasted seeds into a fine powder in a spice grinder. Pour into a small bowl. Add the kosher salt, sugar, garlic, cumin, cloves, nutmeg, chili powder, cayenne pepper and crushed red pepper. Add the oil and molasses, stirring until a paste forms.

Yield: 1 cup seasoning paste

Note:
Use this rub on chicken, shrimp or beef, but pork is where it shines. To use on pork ribs, rinse ribs under cold water and pat dry. Trim off any excess fat. Slit the membrane on the back of the ribs for easier eating. Rub 2 to 3 tablespoons of the paste on each side of a full rack of ribs. Place the ribs on a foil-lined baking sheet. Bake at 350 degrees for 1 to 1 1/2 hours or until cooked through.

Holiday Pork Roast

2 tablespoons dry mustard
2 teaspoons dried thyme
1 (4- to 5-pound) boned rolled pork loin roast
$1/2$ cup sherry
$1/2$ cup soy sauce
2 garlic cloves, minced
1 teaspoon ground ginger
1 (10-ounce) jar red currant jelly
1 tablespoon soy sauce
2 tablespoons sherry

Mix the dry mustard and thyme in a small bowl. Rub over the pork. Place the pork in a large sealable plastic bag. Mix $1/2$ cup sherry, $1/2$ cup soy sauce, the garlic and ginger in a bowl. Pour over the pork and seal the bag. Marinate in the refrigerator for at least 3 hours or overnight, turning the bag occasionally.

Remove the pork and discard the marinade. Place the pork on a rack in a shallow roasting pan. Roast at 350 degrees for $2^{1}/2$ to 3 hours or until a meat thermometer inserted in the thickest part registers 185 degrees. Remove the roast to a cutting board and let stand for at least 5 minutes before carving.

Melt the currant jelly in a small saucepan. Stir in 1 tablespoon soy sauce and 2 tablespoons sherry. Bring to a simmer, stirring occasionally. Serve with the roast.

Yield: 10 to 12 servings

"And the smells from the kitchen! The fat turkey and giblet gravy and cornbread stuffing and sweet potatoes with melted marshmallows and the nectar and ambrosia and roasted pecans and mincemeat pies."

Willie Morris in *"Christmases Gone Revisited" from* Christmas Stories from Mississippi, *edited by Judy H. Tucker and Charline R. McCord*

Jezebel Sauce for Ham

Jezebel sauce is spicy but sweet and is a traditional accompaniment to any cured baked ham (although Mississippi folks are rather partial to Bryan hams). It keeps well in the refrigerator, so it can be made in advance. This also makes a great dipping sauce.

Combine one 12-ounce jar each orange marmalade and apple jelly, 2 teaspoons each prepared horseradish and mustard and 1/2 teaspoon ground ginger in a small saucepan. Cook over low heat until the marmalade and jelly are melted, stirring occasionally. Spread over ham before baking.

Cranberry Pork Roast

1 (3- to 4-pound) boneless pork roast
2 tablespoons olive oil
2 cups red wine
1 cup cranberries, finely chopped
1/4 cup honey
1 teaspoon grated orange zest
2 cinnamon sticks
1/8 teaspoon each ground cloves and ground nutmeg
Salt and pepper to taste

Brown the roast on all sides in hot olive oil in a Dutch oven. Remove from the heat. Whisk the wine, cranberries, honey, orange zest, cinnamon sticks, cloves and nutmeg in a bowl. Season with salt and pepper. Pour over the roast in a baking pan. Cover and bake at 350 degrees for 1 1/2 hours or until cooked through. Remove to a cutting board and let stand for 10 minutes before carving.

Yield: 6 to 8 servings

Photograph for this recipe appears on page 60.

Sausage Casserole

1/4 cup (1/2 stick) butter
6 thick slices potato or egg bread, crusts trimmed and cubed
8 ounces bulk pork sausage, cooked, drained and crumbled
1 1/2 cups (6 ounces) shredded Cheddar cheese
6 eggs
1 cup half-and-half
1 teaspoon each salt and dry mustard

Melt the butter in a 9×13-inch baking dish in the oven. Add the bread cubes and toss gently to coat. Spread in an even layer. Top with the cooked sausage and sprinkle with the cheese. Whisk the eggs, half-and-half, salt and dry mustard in a bowl. Pour over the sausage and cheese. Chill, covered, overnight. Bake, uncovered, at 350 degrees for 40 to 50 minutes or until golden brown and bubbly.

Yield: 8 servings

Deerest Sweet Tenderloin

1/2 cup vegetable oil
1 cup white vinegar
3 tablespoons Worcestershire sauce
3 tablespoons teriyaki marinade
Juice of 1 lemon
2 tablespoons Tony's Creole Seasoning
1 tablespoon garlic salt
1 tablespoon minced garlic
1 tablespoon crushed celery seeds
1 teaspoon pepper
1 venison tenderloin
1 (12-ounce) package sliced bacon
Raspberry Sauce (below)

Combine the oil, vinegar, Worcestershire sauce, teriyaki marinade, lemon juice, Creole seasoning, garlic salt, minced garlic, celery seeds and pepper in a sealable plastic bag. Add the venison and seal the bag carefully. Marinate in the refrigerator for 24 hours, turning the bag occasionally.

Remove the venison and discard the marinade. Cut the venison crosswise into 2-inch-thick slices. Wrap bacon around the edge of each, securing with wooden picks. Grill over hot coals, preferably with hickory chips added for smoke flavor. Cook for 6 minutes per side for medium-rare or to desired doneness. Serve with Raspberry Sauce on the side.

Yield: 6 servings

Raspberry Sauce

1 cup raspberry preserves
1/2 cup red wine

Combine the raspberry preserves and wine in a small nonreactive saucepan. Cook until the preserves are melted and the sauce is hot, stirring frequently.

Yield: 1 1/2 cups

Chicken and Dumplings

1 chicken, cut up
2/3 cup shortening
6 cups self-rising flour
2 tablespoons (about) hot water
1 teaspoon salt
1 teaspoon pepper
1 onion, chopped
1/4 cup (1/2 stick) butter, melted
1 tablespoon sugar

Place the chicken pieces in a large saucepan and add enough water to cover. Simmer over medium heat until cooked through. Remove the chicken and let cool slightly. Reserve 6 cups of the cooking liquid. Remove the chicken from the bones and discard the skin and bones. Cover the chicken and chill.

Cut the shortening into the flour in a bowl until it is the size of peas. Stir in the hot water to make a stiff dough. Roll out half the dough 1/8 inch thick on a floured surface. Cut the dough into 1-inch strips.

Combine the reserved cooking liquid, salt and pepper in a large saucepan. Bring to a rolling boil. Add the dumpling strips 1 at a time. Remove the dumplings to a baking dish as they float to the top. Top the dumplings with the cooked chicken and the onion. Continue cooking the chicken broth until it is reduced to 2 cups. Pour the reduced broth over the chicken and dumplings. Roll out the remaining dough 1/8 inch thick on a floured surface. Fit over the layers. Brush with the melted butter and sprinkle with the sugar. Bake at 375 degrees until golden brown.

Yield: 6 to 8 servings

"My husband and I were enjoying a peaceful afternoon when two ladies unexpectedly came to pay a visit. The afternoon turned into evening and although I only had three pork chops in the refrigerator, I felt that it would be rude not to invite them to stay for supper. I wondered how I was going to serve four people. Then an idea came to me . . . I cut a piece of wheat bread into the shape of a pork chop, put it on the serving platter with the real pork chops and covered them all with gravy. I served everyone a beautiful pork chop, serving myself the last, well-disguised chop!"

Elizabeth Smith Gwin
Class of 1930

Chicken Crepes

1 cup (2 sticks) butter
1 cup all-purpose flour
3 cups chicken broth
2 cups half-and-half
2 1/4 teaspoons salt
1 teaspoon pepper
1/2 teaspoon rubbed sage
2 teaspoons lemon juice
3 cups chopped cooked chicken (about 8 chicken breasts)
1 tablespoon chopped pimento
12 precooked crepes
2 tablespoons grated Parmesan cheese

Melt the butter in a saucepan over low heat. Add the flour. Cook to make a blond roux, stirring constantly (see page 43). Whisk in the chicken broth slowly. Whisk in the half-and-half slowly. Stir in the salt, pepper, sage and lemon juice. Cook until thickened. Pour half the sauce into a bowl. Fold in the chopped chicken and pimento. Spoon an equal amount of chicken filling onto each crepe. Roll the crepes around the filling. Place seam side down in a lightly buttered baking dish. Cover the crepes with the remaining sauce. Sprinkle with the cheese. Bake, covered, at 325 degrees for 30 minutes.

Yield: 6 servings

Coq au Vin

2 tablespoons vegetable oil
1 onion, chopped
5 garlic cloves, chopped
1 cup chopped celery
2 cups sliced mushrooms
2 carrots, julienned
1 cup all-purpose flour
$1/2$ teaspoon each salt, black pepper, celery salt, basil,
    dried thyme, dry mustard, lemon pepper, garlic salt
    and dried parsley flakes
1 large chicken, skin removed and cut up
$3/4$ cup chicken broth
2 cups Burgundy
Hot cooked rice

Heat the oil in a large skillet. Add the onion, garlic, celery, mushrooms and carrots and sauté until brown. Remove the vegetables to a large baking dish. Combine the flour, salt, black pepper, celery salt, basil, thyme, dry mustard, lemon pepper, garlic salt and parsley flakes in a shallow bowl. Add the chicken a few pieces at a time and coat with the flour mixture. Brown the chicken in the same skillet used to cook the vegetables.

Place the chicken on top of the vegetables. Deglaze the skillet with the chicken broth and pour over the chicken. Pour the Burgundy over the top. Bake, covered, at 375 degrees for 1 hour or until the chicken is cooked through. Uncover and bake for 10 minutes. Serve with the rice.

Yield: 4 servings

Lemony Grilled Chicken

1 cup (2 sticks) butter
1 cup fresh lemon juice
3 tablespoons Worcestershire sauce
1/2 cup garlic powder
1 tablespoon salt
5 whole chicken breasts

Combine the butter, lemon juice, Worcestershire sauce, garlic powder and salt in a saucepan. Cook until the butter melts, stirring occasionally. Place the chicken on a grill rack 10 inches above hot coals. Baste the chicken liberally with the butter sauce. Grill for 40 minutes or until the chicken is cooked through, turning every 10 minutes and basting generously with the butter sauce at each turn.

Yield: 5 servings

Mediterranean Chicken

3/4 cup dried prunes, halved and pitted
1/2 cup green olives, pitted
1/2 cup each dry white wine and red wine vinegar
2 tablespoons olive oil
2 tablespoons chopped fresh oregano
5 teaspoons chopped fresh basil
3/4 teaspoon crushed red pepper
3/4 teaspoon salt
3 bay leaves
3/4 cup packed dark brown sugar
6 whole chicken legs

Combine the prunes, olives, white wine, vinegar, olive oil, oregano, basil, crushed red pepper, salt, bay leaves and brown sugar in a bowl. Stir to mix well. Cover and chill overnight.

Arrange the chicken in a baking dish. Pour the prune mixture over the top. Bake at 350 degrees until the chicken is golden brown and cooked through, basting occasionally during cooking.

Yield: 6 servings

"I love to have dinner parties and enjoy having a varied menu, but I always test a new recipe first. You should never serve a dish for the first time at a party. A buffet is a practical way to serve, and I prefer to have a tray for each guest to make the transition from the buffet to the table a little easier. Lightweight, hand-painted trays are practical and beautiful."

Frances Gregory Patterson
Class of 1939

Mandarin Chicken

3 whole chicken breasts, split
Salt and pepper to taste
$1/4$ cup corn oil
$1/2$ cup orange juice
$1/4$ cup soy sauce
1 tablespoon all-purpose flour
1 teaspoon white vinegar
1 teaspoon dry mustard
1 teaspoon onion salt
$1/2$ teaspoon garlic powder
$1/4$ cup pineapple preserves
1 (11-ounce) can mandarin oranges, drained
$1/2$ cup chopped green bell pepper
Hot cooked rice

Season the chicken with salt and pepper. Heat the corn oil in a skillet. Add the chicken and sauté until golden brown. Arrange the chicken in a lightly greased baking dish.

Combine the orange juice, soy sauce and flour in a bowl. Stir until smooth. Stir in the vinegar, dry mustard, onion salt, garlic powder and pineapple preserves. Pour over the chicken. Bake, covered, at 350 degrees for 1 hour or until the chicken is cooked through, basting occasionally. Top with the oranges and bell pepper. Bake, uncovered, for 5 to 8 minutes. Serve over the rice.

Yield: 6 servings

Thomas Ann's Fried Rice

1 tablespoon peanut oil
1 to 1¹/₂ pounds boneless skinless chicken breasts
   (about 3 breasts), chopped
1 bell pepper, julienned
1 onion, thinly sliced
16 ounces mushrooms, sliced
Bean sprouts (optional)
Sliced water chestnuts (optional)
3 or 4 eggs
4 cups cooked white rice, cooled
Soy sauce to taste

Heat a large wok or skillet. Add the peanut oil when hot. Add the chicken when the oil is very hot. Sauté until the chicken is halfway cooked. Add the bell pepper and onion in a ring around the chicken. Cook until the chicken is cooked through.

Stir to mix and form into a ring. Place the mushrooms in the center of the ring. Cook until the mushrooms are tender, mixing gradually. Stir in the bean sprouts and water chestnuts. Form the mixture into a ring. Crack the eggs into the center of the ring and stir to scramble. Keep the other ingredients separated from the eggs until the eggs are cooked through.

Reduce the heat to low. Spoon the cooked rice over the top and sprinkle with soy sauce until the rice is golden brown. Stir to mix. Cook until heated through. Season with additional soy sauce.

Yield: 6 servings

Variation:
Pork and/or shrimp may be substituted for part or all of the chicken.

Sour Cream Baked Chicken Breasts

2 cups sour cream
4 teaspoons Worcestershire sauce
2 teaspoons salt
2 teaspoons paprika
1 teaspoon celery salt
1 teaspoon white pepper
$1/2$ teaspoon garlic powder
$1/4$ cup lemon juice
12 boneless skinless chicken breasts
$1/2$ cup (1 stick) butter, melted
$1^3/4$ cups bread crumbs

Mix the sour cream, Worcestershire sauce, salt, paprika, celery salt, white pepper, garlic powder and lemon juice in a bowl. Dip each piece of chicken in the sour cream mixture to coat and place in a shallow baking dish. Spoon the remaining sour cream mixture evenly over the chicken. Cover with plastic wrap and chill overnight.

Mix the melted butter and bread crumbs in a bowl. Sprinkle over the chicken. Bake at 350 degrees for $1^1/4$ hours or until cooked through.

Yield: 12 servings

Kentucky Chicken

2 cups bread crumbs
1/2 cup (2 ounces) grated Parmesan cheese
1/4 cup fresh parsley, chopped
1 garlic clove, minced
2 teaspoons salt
1/8 teaspoon pepper
3 pounds chicken breasts, boned (about 6 breasts)
1 cup (2 sticks) butter, melted

Mix the bread crumbs, cheese, parsley, garlic, salt and pepper in a shallow bowl. Dip the chicken in the melted butter and then into the bread crumb mixture. Arrange the chicken in a baking pan. Pour the remaining butter over the chicken. Bake at 350 degrees for 1 hour or until the chicken is cooked through, basting frequently with the pan drippings. Do not turn the chicken.

Yield: 6 servings

Baked Catfish Parmesan

2 cups bread crumbs
3/4 cup (3 ounces) grated Parmesan cheese
1/4 cup chopped parsley
2 teaspoons salt
1/2 teaspoon each pepper and dried oregano
1 teaspoon paprika
1/4 teaspoon dried basil
6 catfish fillets
3/4 cup (1 1/2 sticks) butter, melted

Mix the bread crumbs, cheese, parsley, salt, pepper, oregano, paprika and basil in a shallow pan. Dip the fish in the melted butter and then into the bread crumb mixture, pressing to coat evenly. Arrange the fish in a well-greased shallow baking pan. Bake at 375 degrees for 20 to 25 minutes or until the fish flakes easily. Garnish with lemon wedges.

Yield: 6 servings

"Kentucky Chicken was served at many of the special meals. Lynn McCrane Gardner, a graduate of MSCW, shared this recipe with me when we worked together at Auburn University before I became Director of Food Service at The W."

Mary Cecil Forbus
Former Director of MUW Food Service

Catfish with Lemon-Mustard Caper Beurre Blanc

2 tablespoons finely chopped shallots
1/2 cup Champagne vinegar or white wine vinegar
1/4 cup white wine
1 1/2 teaspoons black peppercorns
1 to 2 tablespoons country Dijon mustard
3 cups (6 sticks) butter
2 tablespoons capers
Juice of 1/2 lemon
Salt and pepper to taste
4 catfish fillets
1/2 cup all-purpose flour
1 tablespoon salt
1 tablespoon pepper
1/4 cup (1/2 stick) butter
2 tablespoons olive oil

Combine the shallots, vinegar, wine and peppercorns in a small saucepan. Cook over medium heat until reduced by half. Strain out the shallots and peppercorns and return the liquid to the saucepan. Whisk in the Dijon mustard. Whisk in 3 cups butter 1 tablespoon at a time. Remove the saucepan from the heat occasionally to keep the sauce from getting too hot. Stir in the capers and lemon juice when all the butter is blended. Season with salt and pepper. Keep the sauce warm while cooking the fish.

Rinse the catfish fillets and pat dry. Mix the flour, 1 tablespoon salt and 1 tablespoon pepper in a shallow bowl. Heat 1/4 cup butter and the olive oil in a large skillet. Coat the fish in the flour mixture and shake off any excess. Cook the fillets for 2 to 3 minutes or until golden brown. Turn and cook until the fish flakes easily. Top with the sauce and serve immediately.

Yield: 4 servings

Beer-Battered Catfish

1¹/₂ pounds catfish fillets
1 cup all-purpose flour
1 teaspoon baking powder
1 teaspoon salt
1 tablespoon vegetable oil
1 cup flat beer
¹/₂ teaspoon Tabasco sauce
Peanut oil for frying
Cocktail sauce or tartar sauce

Rinse the catfish fillets and cut into strips. Pat dry with paper towels. Cover and chill. Sift the flour, baking powder and salt into a bowl. Whisk in the vegetable oil, beer and Tabasco sauce. Chill the batter.

Heat 1 inch of peanut oil to 375 degrees in a large heavy skillet. Dip the cold fish into the cold batter to coat. Fry in batches for 4 minutes or until the fish flakes easily, turning occasionally for even browning. Remove to a heatproof plate and keep warm in a 200-degree oven while cooking the remaining fish. Serve with cocktail sauce or tartar sauce.

Yield: 4 servings

Redfish Belvedere

4 (4- to 6-ounce) red fish fillets
2 cups milk
1 cup all-purpose flour
1 teaspoon salt
1 teaspoon black pepper
Garlic salt to taste
Chopped fresh or dried thyme to taste
Chopped fresh or dried basil to taste
Lemon pepper to taste
1/2 cup olive oil
1/2 cup (1 stick) butter
1 cup chopped green onions
5 garlic cloves, minced
Chopped fresh parsley

Marinate the fish fillets in the milk in a shallow bowl for
30 minutes. Drain and discard the milk. Combine the flour, salt
and black pepper on a sheet of waxed paper. Season with garlic
salt, thyme, basil and lemon pepper and stir to mix. Dip the fish
in the flour mixture to coat generously. Heat the olive oil and
butter in a large skillet. Cook the fillets for 5 minutes per side or
until the fish flakes easily. Remove to a plate and keep warm. Add
the green onions and garlic to the skillet. Sauté until tender. Serve
over the fish. Top with chopped parsley.

Yield: 4 servings

Soy-Broiled Salmon

1 (1-pound) salmon fillet
3 tablespoons fresh lemon juice
1 tablespoon soy sauce
1 tablespoon vegetable oil
1 garlic clove, minced
1 teaspoon Worcestershire sauce
1 teaspoon dried basil
1/4 teaspoon pepper

Rinse the salmon and pat dry with paper towels. Place on a lightly oiled rack in a broiler pan. Preheat the broiler. Mix the lemon juice, soy sauce, oil, garlic, Worcestershire sauce, basil and pepper in a large measuring cup or small bowl. Pour half the sauce over the fish. Broil for 5 to 6 minutes. Pour the remaining sauce over the fish and broil for 4 to 5 minutes or until the fish flakes easily. Garnish with lime wedges and serve.

Yield: 2 servings

Old-Fashioned Salmon Croquettes

1 (10-ounce) can salmon
1/4 teaspoon salt
1 egg, beaten
1/2 cup all-purpose flour
1/4 teaspoon baking soda
1/2 cup buttermilk
Vegetable oil for frying

Mix the salmon, salt and egg in a bowl. Sift the flour and baking soda into a small bowl. Add to the salmon mixture and mix. Add the buttermilk and stir to mix. Heat the oil in a large heavy skillet. Drop spoonfuls of the salmon mixture into the oil. Cook until golden brown. Drain on paper towels and serve.

Yield: 2 servings

Snapper with Onions

1 tablespoon butter
1 tablespoon vegetable oil
2 cups thinly sliced onions
All-purpose flour for coating
Chopped fresh thyme or oregano
4 (5- to 6-ounce) snapper fillets
Salt and pepper to taste
$1/4$ cup bread crumbs
1 tablespoon chopped fresh parsley
$1/3$ cup dry white wine

Heat the butter and oil in a skillet. Add the onions and sauté until tender. Remove the onions and set the skillet aside. Season flour with fresh thyme in a shallow bowl. Season the snapper fillets with salt and pepper. Coat the fish in the flour mixture. Heat the skillet used to cook the onions. Add the fish and brown quickly on both sides.

Arrange the fish in a single layer in a baking dish. Top with the cooked onions. Mix the bread crumbs and parsley in a small bowl. Sprinkle over the onions. Pour the wine around the fish. Bake at 350 degrees for 25 to 35 minutes or just until the fish begin to flake, basting occasionally.

Yield: 4 servings

"Just as there are many Souths, there are many Southern cuisines. A blanket definition is all but impossible, though you could build a case that a good portion of Southern cookery is built on a foundation of pork and corn and the interplay of African, European, and Native American traditions. You might also argue that Southern cuisine is a dominant gene, transforming any foodstuff cooked for a long period of time by most any ethnic group into Southern cuisine."

John T. Edge
Director,
Southern Foodways Alliance

Baked Stuffed Lobster

1/4 cup (1/2 stick) unsalted butter
1 medium onion, finely chopped
1 sprig of flat-leaf parsley, chopped
4 ounces deveined peeled shrimp
Salt and freshly ground pepper to taste
2 (1 1/2-pound) live Maine lobsters
17 butter crackers, crumbled
1/4 cup (1/2 stick) unsalted butter, melted

Melt 1/4 cup butter in a saucepan. Add the onion and sauté until tender but not brown. Add the parsley and shrimp and sauté for 1 minute. Remove from the heat and let cool slightly. Season with salt and pepper.

Place the lobster on its back on a work surface. Hold the lobster firmly with one hand and insert the point of a sharp heavy knife where the head meets the body. Slice through the entire length of the body and tail in one quick motion. Spread the lobster open with your hands. Remove and discard the food sac near the head. Remove and reserve the tomalley and eggs, if present. Remove and discard the vein that runs down the middle of the tail. Crack the claws. Rinse the lobster under cold running water and pat dry. Season lightly with salt and pepper. Repeat with the second lobster.

Stir the tomalley and eggs into the shrimp mixture, if desired. Fold in the cracker crumbs gently. Spread the mixture evenly over the center of the lobsters. Brush the tail, stuffing and cracked claws with 1/4 cup melted butter. Place the stuffed lobsters on a baking sheet. Bake at 350 degrees for 18 minutes or until the lobster meat is opaque.

Yield: 2 to 4 servings

Sherried Seafood Casserole

8 ounces king crab meat, flaked
8 ounces deveined peeled cooked shrimp
1 (14-ounce) can artichoke hearts, drained
4 ounces mushrooms, sliced
2 tablespoons lemon juice
$1/2$ cup (2 ounces) shredded Swiss cheese
5 tablespoons butter
5 tablespoons all-purpose flour
$1^1/2$ cups heavy cream
$1/4$ cup dry sherry
1 teaspoon salt
$1/8$ teaspoon white pepper
2 garlic cloves, minced

Layer the crab meat, shrimp, artichoke hearts and mushrooms in a buttered baking dish. Sprinkle with the lemon juice and top with the cheese. Melt the butter in a saucepan. Stir in the flour. Whisk in the cream gradually. Cook until thickened, stirring constantly. Stir in the sherry, salt, white pepper and garlic. Pour over the seafood and vegetables. Bake at 350 degrees for 25 minutes. Garnish with chopped fresh parsley and serve piping hot.

Yield: 4 to 6 servings

Shrimp Salad Niçoise

1 pound deveined peeled medium shrimp
8 ounces small red potatoes
Butter lettuce
12 ounces green beans, trimmed and blanched
20 grape tomatoes
1 small red onion, sliced into thin rings
3 hard-cooked eggs, sliced
1/2 cup small pitted black olives
1/4 cup red wine vinegar
2 tablespoons Dijon mustard
1 1/2 teaspoons chopped fresh basil
1/2 teaspoon salt
1/4 teaspoon black pepper
1/4 teaspoon garlic powder
1/8 teaspoon cayenne pepper
1 cup olive oil

Cook the shrimp in boiling water in a saucepan for 3 to 5 minutes or until the shrimp turn pink; drain and chill. Cook the potatoes in boiling water in a saucepan for 10 minutes or until tender; drain and chill. Arrange lettuce on a serving platter. Arrange the shrimp, potatoes, green beans, tomatoes, onion, eggs and olives on top.

Whisk the vinegar, Dijon mustard, basil, salt, black pepper, garlic powder and cayenne pepper in a bowl. Whisk in the olive oil slowly. Drizzle over the salad.

Yield: 4 servings

Note:
You may arrange the salad on 4 individual plates instead of 1 platter, if desired.

Photograph for this recipe appears on the front cover.

"We study for light to bless with light."

Originally chosen as the motto by The Peyton Literary Society of The W in the 1890s and now to be found on one of the stained glass windows in Orr Chapel and also on The W President's Mace, which is part of the regalia of her office

Green Onion Mayonnaise

6 to 8 green onions,
*   white part only,*
*   very finely chopped*
1 cup thin homemade
*   mayonnaise*

Mix the chopped green onions
and mayonnaise in a bowl.
Cover and chill any excess
for future use.

Yield: 1 cup

Shrimp Belle Bridge

1/4 cup coriander seeds
1 pound deveined peeled medium shrimp
3/4 teaspoon cayenne pepper
1/2 teaspoon salt
2 tablespoons canola oil
Rice wine vinegar
2 tablespoons canola oil
Fresh spring mix salad greens
2 tablespoons Green Onion Mayonnaise (at left)
Freshly grated Parmigiano-Reggiano cheese

Place the coriander seeds in a small skillet. Toast over medium-high heat until they become fragrant, being careful not to burn. Remove from the heat immediately and let cool. Crush coarsely in a spice grinder or with a mortar and pestle.

Blot the shrimp with a paper towel. Mix the crushed coriander, cayenne pepper and salt in a small bowl. Coat the shrimp with the coriander mixture. Heat 2 tablespoons canola oil in a nonstick skillet. Add half the shrimp. Cook for 2 minutes per side, turning only once. Just before removing the skillet from the heat, splash liberally with rice wine vinegar while shaking the pan. Remove the shrimp to paper towels to drain. Wipe out the skillet with paper towels and repeat with 2 tablespoons canola oil and the remaining shrimp.

Toss the salad greens gently with the Green Onion Mayonnaise in a bowl. Arrange on plates. Top with the shrimp and sprinkle with Parmigiano-Reggiano cheese. Serve immediately.

Yield: 2 entrée or 4 appetizer servings

Note:
If using commercially prepared mayonnaise instead of homemade, stir in 1 to 2 tablespoons sour cream or plain yogurt to thin the mayonnaise.

Baked Eggplant with Shrimp

1 medium eggplant, peeled
3 tablespoons all-purpose flour
$1/2$ cup olive oil
$1^1/2$ pounds deveined peeled shrimp
3 large tomatoes, peeled and chopped
Salt and pepper to taste
$3/4$ cup soft bread crumbs
1 tablespoon finely chopped parsley
2 tablespoons minced garlic
$1/4$ teaspoon dried thyme

Cut the eggplant into 1-inch cubes. Toss in the flour to coat. Heat $1/3$ of the olive oil in a skillet until hot. Add $1/2$ of the eggplant. Sauté until tender. Arrange in a baking dish. Repeat with another $1/3$ of the olive oil and the remaining eggplant. Add to the baking dish. Add the remaining olive oil to the skillet and heat until hot. Add the shrimp and sauté until the shrimp turn pink. Arrange on top of the eggplant. Add the tomatoes to the skillet. Simmer for 10 minutes. Season with salt and pepper. Spoon over the shrimp. Mix the bread crumbs, parsley, garlic and thyme in a bowl. Sprinkle on top of the tomato layer. Bake at 400 degrees until golden brown.

Yield: 6 servings

Variation:
You may substitute browned ground beef mixed with Parmesan cheese for the shrimp.

90

Shrimp Curry

5 tablespoons butter
1/2 cup finely chopped onion
6 tablespoons all-purpose flour
1 1/4 teaspoons salt
1/4 teaspoon ginger
1 1/2 teaspoons sugar
2 1/2 teaspoons curry powder
1 cup chicken broth
2 cups milk
4 cups deveined peeled cooked shrimp
1 teaspoon lemon juice
Hot cooked rice

Place the butter in the top of a double boiler. Cook over simmering water until melted. Add the onion and cook until tender. Stir in the flour, salt, ginger, sugar and curry powder. Whisk in the chicken broth and milk gradually. Cook over boiling water until thickened, stirring constantly. Stir in the shrimp and lemon juice. Cook until heated through. Add additional seasoning, if desired. Serve over the rice.

Yield: 4 to 6 servings

Coconut Shrimp

2 eggs, beaten
3 tablespoons lime juice
$1/2$ teaspoon prepared mustard
$1/2$ teaspoon salt
$1/2$ teaspoon cayenne pepper
24 extra-large deveined peeled shrimp
$2/3$ cup all-purpose flour
$1/2$ cup flaked coconut
$1/4$ cup ($1/2$ stick) butter
$1/4$ cup orange marmalade
2 tablespoons prepared mustard
1 teaspoon prepared horseradish
Dash of salt
Dash of turmeric

Mix the eggs, lime juice, $1/2$ teaspoon mustard, $1/2$ teaspoon salt and cayenne pepper in a bowl. Dip the shrimp in the flour and then into the egg mixture. Roll each shrimp in the coconut to coat. Melt the butter in a 10×15-inch baking pan in the oven. Tilt to coat the pan evenly with the melted butter. Arrange the shrimp in the pan. Bake at 450 degrees for 5 minutes. Turn the shrimp over and bake until golden brown outside and pink inside.

Combine the orange marmalade, 2 tablespoons mustard, horseradish, dash of salt and turmeric in a small saucepan. Cook just until heated through and slightly thinned, stirring frequently. Serve on the side with the shrimp.

Yield: 4 servings

Note:
The shrimp may be fried instead of baked if desired.

Marinating is a wonderful way to add flavor to meat or poultry. Marinades usually contain an acidic ingredient, such as wine, citrus juice, or vinegar, along with herbs and spices, a sweetener, and a bit of oil. Even tender cuts of meat can benefit from a judicious use of marinades. Tender meats, such as pork tenderloin, beef fillets, or chicken can become mushy from the acids, however, if left submerged too long. As a general rule, don't leave tender cuts of meat submerged in an acidic marinade for more than 2 hours. And always marinate in a closed container in the refrigerator for safety's sake.

Shrimp Fettuccini

2 cups (4 sticks) butter
1/2 cup white wine (optional)
2 teaspoons minced garlic
2 pounds deveined peeled shrimp, rinsed well
Salt and pepper to taste
16 ounces angel hair pasta, cooked al dente and drained
1/2 cup (2 ounces) grated Parmesan cheese

Melt the butter in a large saucepan. Bring to a simmer and add the wine and garlic. Cook for 1 minute. Add the shrimp and simmer for 2 minutes or until the shrimp turn pink. Season with salt and pepper. Divide the cooked pasta among 6 plates. Spoon the sauce over the pasta and sprinkle with the cheese.

Yield: 6 servings

Marinade for Pork

1/4 cup soy sauce
2 tablespoons dry red wine
1 tablespoon honey
1 tablespoon brown sugar
1 garlic clove, minced
1/2 teaspoon cinnamon
1 green onion, finely chopped

Combine the soy sauce, wine, honey, brown sugar, garlic, cinnamon and green onion in a large sealable plastic bag.

Yield: 1/2 cup marinade

Note:
To use on pork, marinate 2 pounds pork tenderloins or pork loin roast in the refrigerator for 2 hours. Roast or grill the pork as desired, basting every 15 minutes with the marinade. Discard any unused marinade.

Caribe Marinade

1 cup tequila
1 cup soy sauce
$1/4$ cup honey
2 tablespoons lemon juice
2 tablespoons molasses
2 tablespoons chopped fresh cilantro
1 tablespoon chopped fresh gingerroot
$1^1/2$ teaspoons chopped garlic
$1/4$ teaspoon crushed red pepper

Combine the tequila, soy sauce, honey, lemon juice, molasses, cilantro, gingerroot, garlic and crushed red pepper in a large sealable plastic bag.

Yield: $2^1/2$ cups marinade

Note:
To use on beef, marinate 1 ($2^1/2$- to 3-pound) flank steak in the refrigerator for at least 2 hours and preferably overnight. Remove the steak and discard the marinade. Broil or grill the steak as desired. Remove to a cutting board and let stand for 5 minutes before slicing thinly against the grain. This marinade may also be used for chicken, pork, or a meaty fish such as swordfish.

Vegetables and Side Dishes

Whitfield Hall

Old Maid's Gate and Kissing Rock

Young women walking backwards through a gate may appear a bit odd at first, but the students at MUW bow to tradition as they turn to enter the Old Maid's Gate on front campus just as their mothers and grandmothers did before them. The gate was a gift to the school from the Class of 1920. Two date stones sit at each corner: 1884, the year the university was founded, and 1920, the year the gift was made and the year the name changed to Mississippi State College for Women.

This beautiful open concrete structure replaced an iron gate that was chained just before dark each night. An article in the April 30, 1921, campus newspaper commented, "As we look upon this gate, we are reminded that times have changed and that now our girls on entrance are really college women who are no longer to be enchained beings but who, under a wise direction, are capable of prescribing their own moral codes and abiding by them."

It has become a time-honored tradition of "W" students to enter the gate by walking backwards to ensure that their futures hold the spouses of their dreams. Failing to do so can only be remedied and the spell broken by stopping to kiss the Kissing Rock, which sits nearby. The Kissing Rock is inscribed with the dates significant to the opening of the university and was erected May 13, 1935, by the Daughters of the American Revolution.

Sautéed Asparagus

1 pound fresh asparagus
2 tablespoons olive oil
2 garlic cloves, minced
1 teaspoon chopped fresh basil
Salt and lemon pepper to taste

Snap off the tough ends of the asparagus spears. Wash thoroughly in very cold water; drain. Heat a large skillet. Add the olive oil and heat. Add the asparagus and garlic. Sauté until tender-crisp. Sprinkle with the basil and season with salt and lemon pepper. Serve hot.

Yield: 4 servings

Skillet Cabbage

1 cup chopped onion
1 garlic clove, minced
1 1/2 teaspoons grated gingerroot
2 tablespoons butter
4 cups coarsely shredded cabbage
1/2 cup shredded carrot
2 teaspoons soy sauce
1/4 teaspoon freshly ground pepper
1/8 teaspoon paprika (optional)

Sauté the onion, garlic and gingerroot in the butter in a large skillet. Add the cabbage and carrot. Stir-fry over medium-high heat for 5 minutes or until the vegetables are tender-crisp. Sprinkle with the soy sauce, pepper and paprika and serve immediately.

Yield: 4 to 6 servings

"Frozen foods were just becoming commonly used when I started working as Director of Food Service at MUW and most of the selection was confined to vegetables grown in the South and familiar to us, such as turnip greens, carrots, corn, and peas. Broccoli was not, at the time, a part of a Southerner's diet and in an effort to introduce "W" students to new foods, we served broccoli for dinner one evening. It was not received with great enthusiasm, as you can imagine. The students referred to it as trees."

Mary Cecil Forbus
Former Director of Food Services, MUW

Heavenly Green Beans

2 tablespoons butter
1 onion, chopped
1/2 cup packed brown sugar
1 tablespoon vinegar
2 (14-ounce) cans green beans, drained
1/2 cup pecans, chopped
Salt and pepper to taste

Melt the butter in a large skillet. Add the onion and sauté for 3 minutes. Stir in the brown sugar, vinegar, green beans and pecans. Season with salt and pepper. Simmer, covered, over medium heat for 30 minutes.

Yield: 4 to 6 servings

Photograph for this recipe appears on page 60.

Sauce for Broccoli or Green Beans

1/2 cup mayonnaise
2 tablespoons corn oil
1/4 teaspoon dry mustard
1/4 teaspoon Worcestershire sauce
2 hard-cooked eggs, mashed
1 tablespoon finely chopped onion
Dash of Tabasco sauce
Salt to taste

Combine the mayonnaise, corn oil, dry mustard, Worcestershire sauce, mashed eggs, onion and Tabasco sauce in a bowl. Season with salt. Stir to mix well. Toss with hot steamed broccoli or green beans.

Yield: Enough for 3 cups cooked vegetables

Tuscan Beans with Greens

5 tablespoons olive oil
6 garlic cloves, minced
3 tablespoons chopped fresh rosemary, or 1 1/2 teaspoons
   dried rosemary
2 (15-ounce) cans cannellini beans
1/3 bunch fresh turnip greens, cleaned and chopped
Salt and cracked pepper to taste
Chicken broth
8 slices French bread, toasted
Extra-virgin olive oil
Grated Parmesan cheese

Heat the olive oil in a large saucepan. Add the garlic and rosemary and sauté for 1 to 2 minutes. Add the beans and bring to a simmer. Cook for 5 minutes.

Add the turnip greens and cook until wilted, stirring frequently. Season with salt and pepper. Add a small amount of chicken broth to thin the mixture if necessary. Spoon onto the toasted bread and drizzle with olive oil. Sprinkle with cracked pepper and Parmesan cheese.

Yield: 8 servings

Note:
This may be served as a side dish for grilled meat instead of on toasted bread.

Roasted Carrots

12 carrots
3 tablespoons olive oil
1 1/4 teaspoons kosher salt
1/2 teaspoon freshly ground pepper
2 tablespoons finely chopped fresh dill weed or
    flat-leaf parsley
Salt and pepper to taste

Cut the carrots into halves lengthwise only if thick. Cut the carrots diagonally into 1 1/2-inch-thick slices. Toss the carrots, olive oil, salt and pepper in a bowl. Marinate for at least 1 hour. Arrange the marinated carrots in a single layer on a baking sheet. Bake at 400 degrees for 20 minutes. Sprinkle with the dill weed and season with salt and pepper.

Yield: 8 servings

Quick and Spicy Corn Casserole

1 (15-ounce) can whole kernel corn, drained and 1/3 cup
    liquid reserved
1 (15-ounce) can cream-style corn
1/2 cup (1 stick) butter, melted
1 (4-ounce) can green chiles
2 eggs, beaten
1 (8-ounce) package corn muffin mix
1 cup sour cream
2 cups (8 ounces) shredded sharp Cheddar cheese

Combine the reserved corn liquid, whole kernel corn, cream-style corn, melted butter, green chiles, eggs, muffin mix and sour cream in a large bowl. Stir to mix well. Pour the batter into a buttered 9×13-inch baking pan. Top with the shredded cheese. Bake at 350 degrees for 45 minutes or until set.

Yield: 8 servings

Eggplant Creole

1 medium onion, chopped
1 green bell pepper, chopped
1/2 cup (1 stick) butter
1/2 cup uncooked rice
1 large eggplant, peeled and chopped
1 (14-ounce) can diced tomatoes
1 cup beef broth
1/2 teaspoon salt
1/2 teaspoon pepper
1/4 teaspoon dried basil
1/4 teaspoon dried oregano
Tabasco sauce to taste
1 cup (4 ounces) grated Parmesan cheese

Sauté the onion and bell pepper in the butter in a large skillet. Add the rice and sauté until translucent. Stir in the eggplant, tomatoes, beef broth, salt, pepper, basil and oregano. Season with Tabasco sauce. Pour into a buttered 2-quart baking dish. Bake, covered, at 350 degrees for 30 minutes. Sprinkle with the cheese. Bake, uncovered, for 30 minutes longer or until golden brown.

Yield: 8 servings

MUW Alma Mater

*Serene as the dawning
Your promise now unfolds
To new heights of wisdom
Proclaiming truth foretold
With courage undaunted
Honor the challenge,
Guiding your purpose bold.*

*Sing, daughters of our
    Alma Mater,
Oh, sing, and cherish your
    mem'ries forever.
Profound our allegiance,
Secure our belief in God.
This creed of our heritage
Illumines the path untrod.*

Savory Baked Potato Topping

Combine 3 ounces softened cream cheese, 3 tablespoons milk, 1 teaspoon lemon juice, 1/2 teaspoon Worcestershire sauce and 1/2 teaspoon garlic salt in a bowl and blend until smooth. Season with pepper. Serve over piping hot baked potatoes.

Potatoes Romanoff

5 cups cubed peeled potatoes
2 teaspoons salt
2 cups creamed cottage cheese
1 cup sour cream
1/4 cup finely chopped green onions
1 garlic clove, minced
1/2 cup (2 ounces) shredded Cheddar cheese
1/2 teaspoon paprika

Cook the potatoes in boiling water in a saucepan until tender. Drain and rinse quickly under cold water. Sprinkle the salt on the potatoes. Mix the cottage cheese, sour cream, green onions and garlic in a bowl. Fold in the potatoes. Pour into a buttered 1 1/2-quart baking dish. Top with the Cheddar cheese and sprinkle with the paprika. Bake at 350 degrees for 40 to 45 minutes.

Yield: 6 to 8 servings

Spicy Oven-Fried Potatoes

Potatoes
Butter-flavor cooking spray
Paprika
Coarsely ground pepper
Grated fat-free Parmesan cheese (optional)

Scrub potatoes and cut into lengthwise wedges. Cover a baking sheet with foil and coat with cooking spray. Arrange the potatoes in a single layer on the baking sheet. Sprinkle with paprika and pepper. Coat the top of the potatoes with cooking spray. Bake at 350 degrees until the potatoes are tender and golden brown. Sprinkle Parmesan cheese over the hot potatoes and serve immediately.

Yield: variable

Hash Brown Casserole

1/2 cup (1 stick) butter
1/4 cup chopped onion
2 cups cream
1/2 cup milk
2 cups sour cream
1 teaspoon salt
1 teaspoon pepper
2 pounds potatoes, peeled and grated
2 cups (8 ounces) shredded Monterey Jack cheese (optional)

Combine the butter, onion, cream, milk, sour cream, salt and pepper in a saucepan. Bring to a simmer, but do not boil. Combine the potatoes and cheese in a buttered baking dish. Pour the hot milk mixture over the top. Bake at 325 degrees for 1 hour or until tender and golden brown.

Yield: 10 servings

Garlic Mashed Potatoes

8 baking potatoes, peeled and quartered
1 teaspoon salt
1/2 cup (1 stick) butter, softened
3/4 teaspoon salt
3/4 cup half-and-half
3 large garlic cloves, minced
1/2 teaspoon white pepper
1/4 cup chopped fresh parsley

Place the potatoes in a saucepan and add enough cold water to cover. Add 1 teaspoon salt. Bring to a boil. Cover and reduce the heat to a simmer. Cook for 30 minutes or until the potatoes are tender; drain. Beat the potatoes in a large mixing bowl with an electric mixer at medium speed. Beat in the butter, 3/4 teaspoon salt, half-and-half, garlic and white pepper. Stir in the parsley.

Yield: 8 to 10 servings

"Dr. Parkinson (MSCW President) and his wife hosted a formal dinner once a month for the students, and we were required to dress in our formal white uniforms or best blue uniforms. The Parkinsons sat at a different table every month, giving us the opportunity to know them. I loved these dinners; they taught us formal dining etiquette and they were enchanting."

Hyacinth McCormick Hayman
Class of 1935

Sweet Potato Casserole

3 cups mashed cooked sweet potatoes
3/4 cup sugar
1 teaspoon salt
1 teaspoon vanilla extract
1/4 cup (1/2 stick) butter, softened
2 eggs, beaten
1/2 cup raisins (optional)
1 cup packed light brown sugar
1/2 cup all-purpose flour
3/4 cup chopped pecans
1/4 cup (1/2 stick) butter, melted

Combine the mashed sweet potatoes, sugar, salt, vanilla, softened butter, eggs, and raisins in a bowl and mix well. Spoon into a buttered baking dish. Mix the brown sugar, flour, pecans and melted butter in a bowl. Sprinkle on top of the sweet potatoes. Bake at 350 degrees for 25 minutes.

Yield: 6 to 8 servings

Baked Yams with Apricots

1 (16-ounce) can apricot halves
2 pounds red yams, peeled and cut into large chunks
1/2 cup pecans, chopped
3/4 cup packed brown sugar
41/2 teaspoons cornstarch
1/4 teaspoon each cinnamon, nutmeg, cardamom and salt
1/4 cup (1/2 stick) butter

Drain the apricots, reserving 1/2 cup of the juice. Place the yams, apricots and pecans in a buttered baking dish. Bake at 300 degrees for 30 minutes. Mix the brown sugar, cornstarch, cinnamon, nutmeg, cardamom and salt in a saucepan. Stir in the reserved apricot juice. Bring to a boil over medium heat. Boil for 2 minutes, stirring constantly. Add the butter and cook until melted. Pour over the yams, apricots and pecans. Bake at 350 degrees for 25 minutes.

Yield: 10 servings

Spinach Casserole

6 tablespoons butter
6 tablespoons all-purpose flour
2 cups milk
2 teaspoons finely chopped onion
2 teaspoons salt
1/2 teaspoon white pepper
1/2 to 3/4 teaspoon nutmeg
4 (10-ounce) packages frozen chopped spinach, cooked, drained and squeezed dry
4 eggs
2 tablespoons lemon juice

Melt the butter in a large saucepan and stir in the flour. Whisk in the milk gradually. Cook until slightly thickened, stirring constantly. Stir in the onion, salt, white pepper and nutmeg. Add the spinach and mix well. Whisk the eggs and lemon juice in a bowl. Stir into the spinach mixture.

Pour into a 2-quart baking dish. Place the baking dish in a larger baking pan. Add enough hot water to the larger pan to come halfway up the sides of the baking dish. Bake at 375 degrees for 45 minutes or until set.

Yield: 10 to 12 servings

Baked Butternut Squash with Apples

1 medium butternut squash, peeled and cut into
   $1/2$-inch slices
1 medium apple, peeled, cored and thinly sliced
$1/4$ cup packed brown sugar
$1/4$ cup ($1/2$ stick) butter, melted
$11/2$ teaspoons all-purpose flour
$1/2$ teaspoon salt
$1/4$ teaspoon cinnamon
$1/4$ teaspoon nutmeg
$1/4$ teaspoon cardamom (optional)

Arrange a layer of squash slices in a baking dish. Top with a layer of apple slices. Repeat the layers. Mix the brown sugar, melted butter, flour, salt, cinnamon, nutmeg and cardamom in a bowl. Pour over the squash and apples. Bake, covered, at 350 degrees for 30 minutes or until tender.

Yield: 6 servings

The Official Miss Forbus' Squash Casserole

8 yellow squash, sliced
1 cup chopped onion
$1/2$ teaspoon salt
Dash of pepper
1 tablespoon margarine
1 cup bread crumbs
3 eggs, beaten
$3/4$ cup milk
1 cup (4 ounces) shredded cheese

Combine the squash, onion, salt, pepper, margarine and a small amount of water in a saucepan. Cook until the squash is tender; drain well. Mix the cooked squash, bread crumbs, eggs and milk in a bowl. Spoon into a baking dish. Bake at 350 degrees for 25 minutes. Top with the cheese and bake for 5 to 6 minutes longer or until the cheese melts.

Yield: 6 to 8 servings

Squash casseroles are a popular item throughout the South and a great way to use fresh garden squash. These casseroles were also a popular item in The W dining hall, and several alums submitted recipes purporting to be the authentic squash casserole served there. Miss Mary Cecil Forbus, the legendary "W" Director of Food Services, assures us that the following is her official recipe, however.

Squash Dressing

2 cups mashed blanched yellow squash
2^{1}/$_{2}$ cups crumbled corn bread
^{1}/$_{2}$ teaspoon salt
^{1}/$_{4}$ teaspoon pepper
^{1}/$_{4}$ teaspoon sage
1 teaspoon dried parsley flakes
^{1}/$_{2}$ cup (1 stick) butter
^{1}/$_{4}$ cup chopped onion
^{1}/$_{4}$ cup chopped celery
^{1}/$_{4}$ cup chopped green bell pepper
^{1}/$_{4}$ cup sliced mushrooms
1 egg
^{1}/$_{2}$ cup chicken broth
^{1}/$_{2}$ cup milk
^{1}/$_{2}$ cup cream
^{1}/$_{4}$ cup sliced almonds

Combine the squash, corn bread, salt, pepper, sage and parsley flakes in a large bowl and mix well. Melt the butter in a skillet. Add the onion, celery, bell pepper and mushrooms. Sauté until tender but not brown. Add to the squash mixture and toss lightly to mix.

Whisk the egg, chicken broth, milk and cream in a bowl. Add to the squash mixture and stir to mix. Spread in a buttered baking dish and sprinkle with the sliced almonds. Bake at 400 degrees for 40 minutes.

Yield: 8 servings

Fresh Tomato Tart

1 (1-crust) pie pastry
8 ounces mozzarella cheese, shredded
2 tablespoons chopped fresh basil
4 or 5 ripe tomatoes, sliced $1/2$ inch thick
$1/2$ teaspoon salt
$1/4$ teaspoon pepper
2 tablespoons extra-virgin olive oil
$1/4$ cup (1 ounce) grated Parmesan cheese

Line a 10-inch springform pan with the pie pastry. Bake at 400 degrees for 7 minutes. Let cool slightly. Sprinkle with the mozzarella cheese and chopped basil. Arrange the sliced tomatoes evenly on top. Sprinkle with the salt and pepper and drizzle with the olive oil. Sprinkle with the Parmesan cheese.

Bake at 400 degrees for 30 to 40 minutes or until the crust is golden brown and the cheeses are melted. Remove to a wire rack to cool. Garnish with additional chopped basil and serve warm or at room temperature.

Yield: 6 to 8 servings

Photograph for this recipe appears on page 94.

"Want to know if someone is a real Southern belle? Just look in her cupboard. If she's got an iced tea pitcher and a deviled egg plate, you can bet she's as Southern as tomato aspic."

Maryln Schwartz
Former Welty Weekend speaker, in A Southern Belle Primer

We have been eating fried green tomatoes in the South for generations, but the rest of the country discovered this early-summer delicacy from Fannie Flagg's book and blockbuster movie Fried Green Tomatoes. *This recipe is not your usual fried green tomato recipe and is straight from* Fannie Flagg's Original Whistle Stop Café Cookbook.

Fried Green Tomatoes with Milk Gravy

1/4 cup bacon drippings
4 green tomatoes, sliced 1/2 inch thick
2 eggs, beaten
Bread crumbs
All-purpose flour
Milk
Salt
Pepper

Heat the bacon drippings in a large heavy skillet over medium-high heat. Dip the tomato slices in the beaten egg and then in the bread crumbs. Add to the skillet and reduce the heat. Fry the tomatoes slowly until golden brown on both sides. Remove to a serving platter with a slotted spatula and keep warm.

Measure the remaining drippings in the skillet. Stir in 1 tablespoon of flour for each tablespoon of drippings. Cook over low heat for 1 minute, stirring constantly. Add 1 cup milk, 1/2 teaspoon salt and 1/4 teaspoon pepper for each tablespoon of flour used. Cook until thickened, stirring constantly. Pour over the fried tomatoes.

Yield: 4 to 6 servings

Snappy Baked Tomatoes

2 cups chopped seeded peeled tomatoes
1/4 cup seasoned bread crumbs
2 teaspoons finely chopped onion
1 teaspoon salt
1/4 teaspoon paprika
1/4 cup (1/2 stick) butter, melted
1/2 cup (2 ounces) shredded sharp Cheddar cheese
1 egg, beaten

Mix the tomatoes, bread crumbs, onion, salt, paprika, melted butter, cheese and egg in a bowl. Pour into a buttered baking dish. Bake at 375 degrees for 35 minutes.

Yield: 4 to 6 servings

Tomato Gravy

1/4 cup (1/2 stick) butter
1 medium onion, chopped
1 bell pepper, chopped
2 jalapeño chiles, seeded and chopped
2 pounds tomatoes, peeled and chopped
1 teaspoon dried oregano
1 teaspoon salt
1/2 teaspoon pepper

Melt the butter in a saucepan. Add the onion, bell pepper and jalapeño chiles. Sauté until the vegetables are tender. Stir in the tomatoes, oregano, salt and pepper. Simmer to reduce the liquid. Serve over hot cooked rice and top with shredded mozzarella cheese.

Yield: 2 cups gravy

Miss Ethel Summerour was the first licensed dietitian in the state of Mississippi. Each year, Miss Summerour conducted a survey of the freshman class to determine their culinary likes and dislikes. The true Southern soul of the students was reflected in their annual selection of black-eyed peas as their favorite vegetable. One of the students' favorite "vegetables" was Miss Summerour's Black-eyed Peas and Corn Bread Squares with Tomato Topping. Now that is a true Southern dish!

Zucchini Toscana

1/2 cup (1 stick) butter
4 cups sliced unpeeled zucchini
1 cup coarsely chopped onion
2 tablespoons chopped fresh parsley
1 tablespoon chopped fresh basil
2 teaspoons chopped fresh oregano
1/2 teaspoon salt
1/2 teaspoon pepper
2 eggs, well beaten
8 ounces mozzarella cheese, shredded
1 (8-ounce) sheet puff pastry dough, thawed
41/2 teaspoons Dijon mustard
2 tablespoons grated Parmesan cheese

Melt the butter in a large skillet. Add the zucchini and onion. Sauté until the vegetables are tender. Stir in the parsley, basil, oregano, salt and pepper. Remove from the heat. Mix the eggs and mozzarella cheese in a bowl. Add the zucchini mixture and toss to mix well.

Roll out the puff pastry dough 1/8 inch thick on a lightly floured surface. Fit into a 10-inch pie plate. Spread with the Dijon mustard. Pour the zucchini mixture into the pie shell and sprinkle with the Parmesan cheese. Bake at 375 degrees for 18 to 20 minutes or until golden brown. Remove to a wire rack and let cool before cutting.

Yield: 8 servings

Photograph for this recipe appears on page 94.

Sherried Fruit Casserole

3 oranges, unpeeled, halved and thinly sliced
1 (29-ounce) can sliced peaches, drained and cut into
    bite-size pieces
1 (29-ounce) can sliced pears, drained and cut into
    bite-size pieces
1 (20-ounce) can pineapple chunks, drained
1 (6-ounce) jar maraschino cherries, drained
1/4 cup (1/2 stick) butter
1/2 cup all-purpose flour
1/2 cup sherry
2/3 cup sugar
1/2 teaspoon salt
1/2 cup packed brown sugar

Place the orange slices in a nonreactive saucepan and barely cover with water. Bring to a simmer. Cook for 20 minutes or until the oranges are tender and most of the water has evaporated. Add the peaches, pears, pineapple and maraschino cherries. Melt the butter in a small saucepan. Stir in the flour, sherry, sugar and salt. Add to the fruit and stir to mix well.

Pour into a buttered 9×13-inch baking dish and sprinkle with the brown sugar. Bake at 350 degrees for 1 hour or until thickened. Serve as a side dish with roast pork, game or turkey or as a topping for ice cream or pound cake.

Yield: 8 servings

Noodle Pudding

3 eggs
1/4 cup packed brown sugar
1/4 teaspoon nutmeg
4 cups cooked wide egg noodles
1/2 cup raisins
1/2 cup sliced almonds
1 tablespoon lemon juice
1/4 cup (1/2 stick) butter, melted
1 tablespoon bread crumbs

Beat the eggs and brown sugar in a mixing bowl until fluffy. Fold in the nutmeg, noodles, raisins, almonds, lemon juice and melted butter. Pour into a buttered baking dish. Sprinkle with the bread crumbs. Bake at 375 degrees for 50 minutes or until piping hot.

Yield: 6 to 8 servings

Dr. Hunt's Cheese Grits

4 cups water
1 cup grits
2 teaspoons salt
2 (5-ounce) packages boursin cheese
1/2 cup (1 stick) butter
6 eggs, beaten

Bring the water to a boil in a saucepan. Stir in the grits and salt and reduce the heat. Cook for 5 to 7 minutes, stirring occasionally. Stir in the cheese and butter and cook until melted. Remove from the heat and cool to lukewarm. Stir in the eggs. Pour into a buttered baking dish. Bake at 350 degrees for 45 minutes.

Yield: 6 servings

Creole Rice

1/4 cup vegetable oil
1 cup uncooked white rice
1/4 cup finely chopped onion
Salt and pepper to taste
1 (15-ounce) can diced tomatoes
1 cup pimento-stuffed green olives, sliced
11/2 cups boiling water

Heat the oil in an ovenproof skillet. Add the rice and onion and sauté until translucent but not brown. Season with salt and pepper. Stir in the tomatoes, olives and boiling water. Bake, tightly covered, at 375 degrees for 45 to 60 minutes or until the liquid is absorbed. Fluff the rice before serving.

Yield: 6 servings

Grits Soufflé

7 cups water
21/2 teaspoons salt
2 cups uncooked grits
6 ounces each Cheddar and Gouda cheese, shredded
1/2 cup (1 stick) butter, cut into pieces
4 egg yolks
1/2 cup milk
1 teaspoon pepper
4 egg whites
Pinch of cream of tartar

Bring the water to a boil in a saucepan. Stir in the salt and grits and reduce the heat to low. Cook until thickened, stirring occasionally. Stir in the Cheddar cheese, Gouda cheese, butter, egg yolks, milk and pepper and cook until the cheeses melt. Remove from the heat and let cool to lukewarm. Beat the egg whites and cream of tartar in a mixing bowl until stiff peaks form. Fold gently into the grits mixture. Pour into a 3-quart baking dish. Bake at 350 degrees for 1 hour.

Yield: 8 to 10 servings

115

"Shattuck Dining Hall at MSCW was a classroom with lessons as important as those learned in mathematics and biology. We learned punctuality (since those who were even a minute late missed the meal entirely). We learned proper manners and social skills with the family-style dining. We learned reverence and patience since we always had a blessing before we served our plates. We learned to appreciate our own Southern cooking culture, even those of us not accustomed to spoon bread and grits."

Lenore Loving Prather
Class of 1953
Former Chief Justice of the Mississippi Supreme Court
Interim President of MUW, 2001-2002

Breads

Culinary Arts Institute, Shattuck Hall

Zouave

One of the most memorable of "W" traditions was the Zouave Marching Drill, which was begun by Miss Emma Ody Pohl, Director of Physical Education at The W from 1907 until 1955. In 1912 Miss Pohl created the drill, which was based on French military routines, for her students. It grew in importance from an exercise for a few students in 1912 to a campus-wide extravaganza that drew crowds of visitors by the time of her retirement in 1955.

The drill was a twenty-minute exhibition of great physical precision, presented as a part of commencement exercises that required many hours of practice to do correctly. It consisted of a presentation of the colors while stirring martial music played, followed by marching and fencing routines performed while the marchers sang "Hail to Thee." The students were attired in short-sleeved white shirts, navy blue shorts, white shoes, and a red sash that went over one shoulder and then circled the waist. After Miss Pohl retired in 1955, the Zouave drill was discontinued, but it has been revived on a much smaller scale on several occasions since the late 1970s to very appreciative audiences.

Never-Fail Dinner Rolls

2 cups milk
1/2 cup shortening
1/2 cup sugar
2 envelopes dry yeast
3/4 cup warm water
3 to 4 cups all-purpose flour
1 tablespoon salt
1 teaspoon baking powder
1/2 teaspoon baking soda
Melted butter

Combine the milk, shortening and sugar in a saucepan. Bring to a boil. Pour into a large bowl and let cool to lukewarm. Dissolve the yeast in the warm water in a small bowl. Let stand until foamy. Stir into the lukewarm milk mixture. Beat in just enough flour to make a cake-like batter.

Let rise in a warm place for 1 1/2 hours. Stir in the salt, baking powder and baking soda. Stir in enough additional flour to make a stiff dough. Roll into balls and arrange in a greased baking pan. Brush with melted butter.

Let rise in a warm place for 1 1/2 hours or until doubled in bulk. Bake at 350 degrees for 25 minutes or until golden brown. Remove to a wire rack to cool.

Yield: 3 dozen rolls

Note:
The rolls may be covered and chilled for several hours after rising and before baking.

An enchanting chapter entitled "Simple Rules for Serving Daintily," from a 1906 II&C cookbook, suggests the following serving tip: "It is a prettier custom to use two small bread plates than one large one heavily laden. For breakfast and luncheon cut the bread in thin slices and lay upon an immaculate doily on the bread plate."

Butterhorn Rolls

4 cups all-purpose flour
4 envelopes dry yeast
1 teaspoon salt
$^1/_3$ cup sugar
1 cup milk
$^1/_2$ cup (1 stick) butter
2 eggs
Butter, softened
Melted butter

Combine 1 cup of the flour, the yeast, salt and sugar in a large mixing bowl. Heat the milk and $^1/_2$ cup butter to 130 degrees in a saucepan. Add to the dry ingredients and beat for 2 minutes with an electric mixer at medium speed. Add $^1/_2$ cup flour and the eggs. Beat for 2 minutes at high speed.

Switch to the dough hook and beat in the remaining $2^1/_2$ cups flour. Place the dough in a greased bowl and brush the surface with softened butter. Let stand in a warm place for 30 minutes or until it begins to rise. Cover and chill for several hours or overnight.

Knead the dough on a floured work surface until smooth and elastic. Divide the dough into 3 equal portions. Roll each into an 8-inch circle and brush with melted butter. Cut into 12 wedges; roll up from the wide ends. Place on a baking sheet and cover. Let rise in a warm place until doubled in bulk. Bake at 350 degrees for 15 minutes. Remove to a wire rack and brush with additional melted butter.

Yield: 3 dozen rolls

Photograph for this recipe appears on the cover.

Mississippi. Feels Like Coming Home

*Have you ever been kissed
 by a warm gulf breeze?
Sipped ice tea beneath
 magnolia trees?
Or sat on the porch and
 just talked a while?
Then I know a place that
 will make you smile.*

*From the hills down to the
 Delta, Jackson's skyline
to the pines, there's a place
 I know, so come on.
Mississippi. Feels like
 coming home.*

*She can tell you stories,
 she can sing you songs.
Feed you like your mama,
 and walk you home.
Show you sights like
 you've never known.*

*Mississippi. Feels like
 coming home.*

Raphael Semmes
*Mississippi Musician and
Songwriter*

Brown Beer Bread

3 cups all-purpose flour
3 cups whole wheat flour
3 tablespoons baking powder
1 tablespoon salt
2/3 cup packed brown sugar
2 (12-ounce) bottles brown beer (such as an ale or bock)

Sift the all-purpose flour, whole wheat flour, baking powder, salt and brown sugar into a bowl. Stir in the beer. Divide the batter between 2 lightly greased loaf pans. Bake at 350 degrees for 40 to 50 minutes or until firm and golden brown. Cool in the pans for 10 minutes. Remove to a wire rack to cool completely.

Yield: 2 loaves

White Bread

From Industrial Institute & College, II&C

1/2 teaspoon salt
1 teaspoon sugar
1 teaspoon shortening
1/2 cup hot water
1/2 cup scalded milk
2 envelopes dry yeast
1/4 cup lukewarm water
3 cups bread flour

Combine the salt, sugar and shortening in a bowl. Stir in the hot water and scalded milk. Cool to lukewarm. Dissolve the yeast in the lukewarm water in a small bowl. Add to the milk mixture. Stir in enough of the bread flour to make a batter. Beat until well mixed. Beat in the remaining flour gradually to make a stiff dough. Knead on a floured work surface until smooth and elastic. Let rise, covered, in a greased bowl in a warm place for 2 to 3 hours or until doubled in bulk. Knead on a floured surface until smooth. Shape into a loaf or rolls. Let rise, covered, in a greased pan until doubled in bulk. Bake at 375 degrees for 50 minutes or until golden brown. Remove to a wire rack to cool.

Yield: 1 loaf or 18 rolls

"The simplest and cheapest of these Southern country delicacies is the mayonnaise sandwich. You take two pieces of bread and liberally smear on them the condiment of the gods. Pretend there's something else in there if you want to, but it's not necessary: It's the mayonnaise that makes most sandwiches taste good anyway."

Paul Ruffin
Former Welty Weekend speaker, from his column "Ruffin It"

Ada's Fig Preserves

Mix 6 cups sugar, 2 cups light corn syrup and 1/4 cup hot water in a saucepan. Bring to a boil. Add 5 pints peeled figs a few at a time, maintaining the liquid at a boil. Boil until the mixture is thickened, stirring frequently. Remove from the heat and let stand for 8 hours. Bring to a boil and boil until the desired consistency, stirring frequently. Pour into hot sterilized jelly jars; seal with 2-piece lids. Process in a boiling water bath for 5 minutes.

Whole Wheat Bread

From Industrial Institute & College, II&C

1 envelope dry yeast
1/4 cup lukewarm water
2 cups milk
2 cups boiling water
1 tablespoon butter
1 tablespoon sugar
2 teaspoons salt
7 to 8 cups whole wheat flour
Melted butter

Stir the yeast into the lukewarm water in a small bowl. Let stand until foamy. Combine the milk, boiling water, 1 tablespoon butter, sugar and salt in a large bowl. Let cool to lukewarm. Stir in the dissolved yeast and enough of the flour to make a thick batter. Whisk until light and spongy.

Cover and let rise in a warm place until doubled in bulk. Stir in enough of the remaining flour to make a stiff dough. Knead on a floured work surface until smooth and elastic. Place the dough in a greased bowl and cover.

Let rise in a warm place until doubled in bulk. Turn the dough out onto a floured work surface and shape into loaves. Place in well-greased loaf pans. Let rise until doubled in bulk. Brush the loaves with melted butter. Bake at 375 degrees for 45 minutes. Remove from the pans. Cool on a wire rack.

Yield: 3 loaves

German Coffee Bread

From Industrial Institute & College, II&C

2 envelopes dry yeast
1/4 cup lukewarm water
1/4 cup sugar
1 cup scalded milk
3 to 4 cups bread flour
1/2 teaspoon salt
1/3 cup shortening, melted
1 egg, beaten
1/2 cup raisins, soaked in hot water to plump
3 tablespoons butter, melted
1/3 cup sugar
1 teaspoon cinnamon
3 tablespoons all-purpose flour
1 egg, beaten

Dissolve the yeast in the lukewarm water in a small bowl.
Combine 1/4 cup sugar and the scalded milk in a large bowl. Let
cool to lukewarm. Stir in the dissolved yeast and enough of the
bread flour to make a batter. Cover and let rise in a warm place
until doubled in bulk. Stir in the salt, melted shortening, 1 egg
and drained raisins. Stir in enough of the remaining bread flour
to make a soft dough. Cover and let rise in a warm place until
doubled in bulk. Spread the dough about 1 inch thick in a
buttered 9×13-inch baking pan. Cover and let rise in a warm
place until doubled in bulk.

   Mix the melted butter, 1/3 cup sugar, cinnamon and
all-purpose flour in a bowl. Brush the dough with 1 beaten egg
when ready to bake. Cover with the cinnamon mixture. Bake at
375 degrees for 30 minutes. Remove to a wire rack to cool.

   Yield: 15 servings

Cinnamon Coffee Cake

2^1/2 cups all-purpose flour
2 cups packed brown sugar
1 teaspoon cinnamon
^{1}/2 teaspoon salt
^{1}/2 cup shortening
1 teaspoon baking powder
^{1}/2 teaspoon baking soda
1 egg
^{3}/4 cup buttermilk

Mix the flour, brown sugar, cinnamon and salt in a large bowl. Cut in the shortening with a pastry blender or fork until crumbly. Remove ^{3}/4 cup and set aside. Add the baking powder and baking soda to the remaining crumb mixture and stir to mix.

Stir the egg and buttermilk in a small bowl. Add to the crumb mixture and mix well. Pour into a well-greased 9-inch cake pan and top with the reserved crumbs. Bake at 350 degrees for 20 minutes or until a wooden pick inserted in the center comes out clean. Cut into wedges and serve piping hot.

Yield: 8 servings

"At a grocery store on (Manhattan's) Upper West Side called Gourmet Garage, I came upon a tray full of cold Krispy Kremes for sale beneath a sign that read, 'Fresh from the Antebellum South.' 'Well now,' I said to the man behind the counter. 'They can't be any too fresh.'"

Roy Blount, Jr.
Former Welty Weekend speaker

Rose's Mexican Spoon Bread

2 tablespoons vegetable oil
1 cup cornmeal
1/2 teaspoon baking soda
1/2 teaspoon salt
1 cup milk
1 (15-ounce) can cream-style corn
2 cups (8 ounces) shredded Cheddar cheese
1/2 cup vegetable oil
1 cup chopped onion
2 jalapeño chiles, seeded and chopped
2 tablespoons pepper jelly
2 eggs, beaten
1 garlic clove, minced

Heat 2 tablespoons oil in a 9-inch cast-iron skillet in a 375-degree oven. Combine the cornmeal, baking soda, salt, milk, corn, cheese, 1/2 cup oil, onion, jalapeño chiles, pepper jelly, eggs and garlic in a large bowl. Stir to mix well.

Pour the batter into the hot skillet and immediately return to the oven. Bake at 375 degrees for 45 to 55 minutes or until golden brown.

Yield: 6 to 8 servings

Corn Bread

2 cups yellow cornmeal
1 cup self-rising flour
3 eggs
1/2 cup mayonnaise
Water

Sift the cornmeal and flour into a bowl. Stir in the eggs and mayonnaise. Add just enough water to make a thick paste and mix well. Spread in an 8-inch square baking pan. Bake at 375 degrees for 25 minutes or until the top is golden brown and a wooden pick inserted in the center comes out clean.

Yield: 6 servings

Hush Puppies

1 cup self-rising cornmeal
1 tablespoon all-purpose flour
1/8 teaspoon salt
1/8 teaspoon sugar
1 onion, chopped
1/2 cup milk
1 egg
Vegetable oil for frying

Combine the cornmeal, flour, salt, sugar, onion, milk and egg in a bowl. Stir to mix well. Let stand for 5 minutes. Heat 1 inch of oil in a large heavy skillet. Drop spoonfuls of batter into the hot oil and cook until golden brown, turning once. Drain briefly on paper towels and serve hot.

Yield: 12 to 16 hush puppies

Cranberry Pecan Bread

2 cups all-purpose flour
1 cup sugar
1 1/2 teaspoons baking powder
1/2 teaspoon baking soda
1/2 teaspoon salt
1/4 cup shortening
3/4 cup orange juice
1 tablespoon finely grated orange zest
1 egg, beaten
1/2 cup chopped pecans
2 cups cranberries, coarsely chopped

Sift the flour, sugar, baking powder, baking soda and salt into a large bowl. Cut in the shortening with a pastry blender or fork until crumbly. Mix the orange juice, orange zest and egg in a bowl. Add to the dry ingredients and mix just until combined. Fold in the pecans and cranberries.

Spoon the batter into a well-greased loaf pan. Bake at 350 degrees for 1 hour and 20 minutes or until a wooden pick inserted in the center comes out clean. Cool in the pan for 10 minutes. Remove to a wire rack to cool completely.

Yield: 1 loaf

Baking powder and baking soda are both used to leaven quick breads such as biscuits, muffins, and scones. Under the right conditions they both produce carbon dioxide gas, but these products cannot be substituted for each other. Baking powder produces carbon dioxide gas when it reacts to moisture and heat, but baking soda reacts only when combined with an acid such as sour cream, buttermilk, or fruit juice. These are simple acid-base reactions at work—and you thought you'd never need chemistry again!

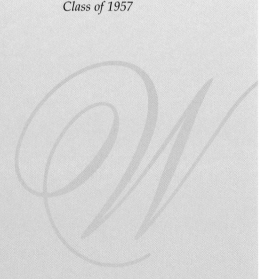

Poppy Seed Bread

3 cups all-purpose flour
1^1/$_2$ teaspoons salt
1^1/$_2$ teaspoons baking powder
2^1/$_4$ cups sugar
1 cup plus 2 tablespoons canola oil
3 eggs
1^1/$_2$ teaspoons vanilla extract
1^1/$_2$ teaspoons almond extract
1^1/$_2$ teaspoons butter flavoring
2 tablespoons poppy seeds
1^1/$_2$ cups milk
Glaze (below)

Sift the flour, salt and baking powder into a bowl. Beat the sugar and canola oil in a large bowl. Add the eggs 1 at a time, beating well after each addition. Stir in the vanilla, almond extract, butter flavoring and poppy seeds. Beat in the dry ingredients alternately with the milk. Pour the batter into 2 greased loaf pans. Bake at 300 degrees for 1 to 1^1/$_2$ hours. Place on a wire rack and let cool for 5 minutes. Pour the Glaze over the bread while still in the pans.

Yield: 2 loaves

Orange Glaze

^{1}/$_2$ cup orange juice
^{1}/$_2$ teaspoon vanilla extract
^{1}/$_2$ teaspoon almond extract
^{1}/$_2$ teaspoon butter flavoring
^{3}/$_4$ cup confectioners' sugar

Combine the orange juice, vanilla, almond extract, butter flavoring and confectioners' sugar in a bowl. Stir until smooth.

Yield: ^{3}/$_4$ cup

"Those of you who had the chance to eat in the dining hall when Miss Summerour was our dietitian remember that she made homemade bread for our meals. On spring afternoons while the bread was baking, we could smell it from our music rooms. Many a day some of us would sidle up to the back door of Shattuck and beg for a piece of hot bread. We were never refused, and it always came with a big pat of butter in the center. My memories of that smell are still quite vivid!"

Donette Dunaway Lee
Class of 1957

Pumpkin Bread

3 cups all-purpose flour
1 teaspoon cinnamon
1 teaspoon allspice
1 teaspoon cloves
1 teaspoon nutmeg
1 teaspoon baking powder
$1/2$ teaspoon baking soda
$1/2$ teaspoon salt
1 cup canola oil
3 cups sugar
3 eggs, beaten
1 teaspoon vanilla extract
1 cup chopped pecans
1 (16-ounce) can pumpkin

Sift the flour, cinnamon, allspice, cloves, nutmeg, baking powder, baking soda and salt into a bowl. Stir the canola oil, sugar, eggs and vanilla in a large bowl. Add the dry ingredients and mix well. Fold in the pecans and pumpkin.

Pour the batter into a greased and floured 9-inch bundt pan. Bake at 325 degrees for $1^1/2$ hours or until a wooden pick inserted in the center comes out clean. Cool in the pan for 10 minutes. Remove to a wire rack to cool completely.

Yield: 12 servings

"Don't get me started on biscuits. That is one subject on which I can hold forth tirelessly, and more than once I've cleared a room with a passionate defense of the crusty-all-over school or a thoughtful discourse on the merits of vegetable shortening. Just for the record, you're not talking to any armchair biscuit-head here. My opinions are backed up by years of solid experience in the field. To be blunt, I have eaten more biscuits than you have."

Stephen Harrigan
in Texas Monthly

Banana Nut Bread

1 cup (2 sticks) butter, softened
1 cup sugar
2 eggs, well beaten
2 cups all-purpose flour
1 teaspoon baking soda
1 teaspoon baking powder
1 cup chopped nuts
3 ripe bananas, mashed

Cream the butter, sugar and eggs in a large mixing bowl until light and fluffy. Sift the flour, baking soda and baking powder into a bowl. Add to the butter mixture and stir to mix well. Fold in the nuts and mashed bananas. Divide the batter between 2 well-greased loaf pans. Bake at 300 degrees for 1 hour or until a wooden pick inserted in the center comes out clean. Cool in the pans for 10 minutes. Remove to a wire rack to cool completely.

Yield: 2 loaves

Buttermilk Biscuits

2 cups all-purpose flour
1 tablespoon baking powder
1/2 teaspoon baking soda
1 teaspoon salt
1/2 cup shortening
1 cup buttermilk

Mix the flour, baking powder, baking soda and salt in a bowl. Cut in the shortening with a pastry blender or fork until the mixture resembles cornmeal. Add the buttermilk and mix just until combined. Knead the dough gently on a floured work surface for a short time. Roll out the dough to 1/2 inch thick. Cut with a 2-inch biscuit cutter. Arrange the biscuits close together on a greased baking sheet. Bake at 450 degrees for 12 to 15 minutes. Remove to a wire rack to cool.

Yield: 20 biscuits

Yeast Biscuits

6 cups all-purpose flour
1/2 cup sugar
1 tablespoon salt
1/2 cup shortening
2 envelopes dry yeast
1 cup lukewarm water
2 cups buttermilk
All-purpose flour

Mix 6 cups flour, the sugar and salt in a bowl. Cut in the shortening with a pastry blender or fork until the mixture resembles coarse cornmeal. Dissolve the yeast in the lukewarm water in a bowl. Stir into the flour mixture. Add the buttermilk and mix well. Pinch off pieces of dough and roll in additional flour. Shape into balls and place each ball in a lightly greased muffin cup. Let rise in a warm place for 30 minutes. Bake at 375 degrees for 20 minutes or until golden brown. Cool in the pan for 5 minutes. Remove to a wire rack to cool completely.

Yield: 40 biscuits

Note:
The dough can be covered and chilled for up to 10 days before baking.

Self-rising flour is popular in the South, where it is used in fluffy biscuits and light-as-air pancakes. It is a blend of flour, salt, and baking powder. Do not substitute regular all-purpose flour for self-rising, or vice versa. An acceptable substitute for self-rising flour can be made by stirring 1/2 teaspoon salt and 1 1/2 teaspoons baking powder into 1 cup regular all-purpose flour.

Carrot Muffins

2 cups all-purpose flour
2 teaspoons baking powder
$^1/_2$ teaspoon salt
2 teaspoons cinnamon
$1^1/_4$ cups sugar
$1^1/_2$ cups canola oil
3 eggs
2 teaspoons vanilla extract
2 cups grated carrots
2 cups raisins

Sift the flour, baking powder, salt and cinnamon into a large bowl. Make a well in the center of the dry ingredients and pour in the sugar, canola oil, eggs and vanilla. Stir until well blended. Fold in the grated carrots and raisins. Fill greased and floured muffin cups half full. Bake at 300 degrees for 20 minutes or until a wooden pick inserted in the center comes out clean. Cool in the pan for 5 minutes. Remove to a wire rack to cool completely.

Yield: 18 muffins

Tea Scones with Devonshire Cream

2 cups all-purpose flour
1/4 cup sugar
2 1/2 teaspoons baking powder
1/2 teaspoon salt
6 tablespoons chilled butter
1 egg, beaten
Buttermilk
1/2 cup chopped dried fruit such as cranberries, apricots,
    currants or raisins
1/2 cup shaved white chocolate
Devonshire Cream (at right)

Sift the flour, sugar, baking powder and salt into a bowl. Cut in the butter with a pastry blender or fork until crumbly. Pour the beaten egg into a 1-cup measuring cup. Add enough buttermilk to equal 1 cup. Stir into the flour mixture. Add the dried fruit and white chocolate and stir to mix.

Drop spoonfuls of batter onto an ungreased baking sheet; or pat into 2 large circles on a floured work surface, cut into wedges and place on an ungreased baking sheet. Bake at 400 degrees for 12 to 15 minutes. Remove to a wire rack to cool. Serve with Devonshire Cream.

Yield: 3 dozen scones

Devonshire Cream

Combine 8 ounces softened cream cheese, 1/2 cup sour cream and 2 tablespoons confectioners' sugar in a bowl and beat until smooth. Cover and chill overnight.

Desserts

Front Parlor at Puckett House

The Goose

The Goose, also know as the Golden Goose Tearoom, has been the traditional campus gathering spot for decades. The popular tearoom acquired its name in 1918, when Miss Ann Barringer, Director of Normal Arts, won a contest to name the new campus café. The Goose served a twofold purpose: to provide students with a place to enjoy inexpensive food and drinks in a casual setting and to raise revenue for the Student Activities Building Fund.

Many a romance began in the Goose as it was the only place during the Parkinson administration (1932-1952) that students could go with a date unchaperoned. Local and Mississippi State boys were often to be found there, competing for the attention of "W" girls.

Located since 1961 in the Hogarth Student Center, the Goose has had several homes throughout the years. Its first home was in the basement of Columbus Hall. It moved in 1927 to the ground floor of the Student Activities Building, which was located where the gazebo now stands. While located there, the Goose was set up in traditional tearoom fashion with table service. After it moved to the Hogarth Student Center, the updated Goose was set up as a snack bar. The Goose was renovated in the mid-1990s as a daytime facility with a companion facility next door called Ody's, which serves students in the evenings.

Fresh Apple Cake

1 cup vegetable oil
2 cups sugar
2 eggs
1 teaspoon vanilla extract
3 cups cake flour
1 tablespoon baking powder
1 teaspoon salt
3 cups chopped cored peeled apples
1 cup chopped pecans or raisins (optional)
1 cup packed brown sugar
1/4 cup milk
1/2 cup (1 stick) butter

Whisk the oil, sugar, eggs and vanilla in a large bowl. Sift the flour, baking powder and salt into a bowl. Add to the sugar mixture. Stir to mix well. Fold in the apples and pecans. Pour the batter into a greased and floured 10-inch tube pan with a removable bottom. Bake at 350 degrees for 45 to 60 minutes or until a wooden pick inserted in the center comes out clean. Remove the pan to a wire rack.

Heat the brown sugar, milk and butter in a saucepan until the butter melts. Bring to a boil. Cook for exactly 3 minutes. Pour the hot sauce over the hot cake in the pan. Let cool for 2 hours. Loosen from the side of the pan with a sharp knife and remove the bottom. Place on a serving plate.

Yield: 16 servings

Mrs. Porter's New Southern Cookery Book, *published in 1871, devotes twice as many pages to desserts as to all the remaining recipes combined. It includes over 200 cake recipes alone, many with fancy names like "Ancient Maiden's Cake." Not wanting to waste precious sugar, however, she notes that "if the ancient maiden's matrimonial prospects are good, frost or ice (the cake) with icing of proper flavor, otherwise serve plain."*

Banana Cake

3 cups all-purpose flour
2 teaspoons baking soda
$2^1/_2$ teaspoons cinnamon
$1^1/_2$ teaspoons cloves
$^1/_2$ teaspoon salt
$^1/_2$ cup (1 stick) butter, softened
$^1/_2$ cup vegetable oil
2 cups sugar
4 eggs
6 bananas, mashed
2 cups chopped pecans
$^1/_2$ cup chopped raisins
$^1/_2$ pound candied cherries (optional)
All-purpose flour

Sift 3 cups flour, the baking soda, cinnamon, cloves and salt into a bowl. Cream the butter, oil and sugar in a mixing bowl until light and fluffy. Add the eggs 1 at a time, beating well after each addition.

Beat in the flour mixture alternately with the bananas. Combine the pecans, raisins and cherries in a bowl. Sprinkle with additional flour and toss to coat lightly. Stir into the cake batter. Pour into a greased and floured tube pan or bundt pan. Bake at 325 to 350 degrees for 1 hour or until a wooden pick inserted in the center comes out clean. Cool in the pan for 10 minutes. Invert onto a serving plate.

Yield: 16 servings

Caramel Cake

1/2 cup (1 stick) butter, softened
11/2 cups sugar
4 eggs
21/2 cups self-rising flour
1 cup half-and-half
2 tablespoons vanilla extract
Cora Mae's Caramel Icing (below)

Cream the butter and sugar in a large mixing bowl until light and fluffy. Add the eggs 1 at a time, beating well after each addition. Beat in the flour alternately with the half-and-half. Fold in the vanilla. Divide the batter between 2 greased 8-inch cake pans. Bake at 325 degrees for 35 minutes or until a wooden pick inserted in the center comes out clean. Cool in the pans for 10 minutes. Remove to a wire rack to cool completely. Spread Cora Mae's Caramel Icing between the layers and over the top and side of the cake.

Yield: 12 servings

Cora Mae's Caramel Icing

21/4 cups sugar
1 cup whipping cream
1 tablespoon light corn syrup
1 cup (1/2 stick) butter or margarine
1 teaspoon vanilla extract

Brown 1/4 cup of the sugar in an iron skillet, and at the same time, bring the whipping cream, remaining sugar and corn syrup to a boil in a 3-quart pan. Add the browned sugar to the boiling liquid. Cook to soft-ball stage. Remove from the heat, and add the butter or margarine and vanilla. Beat at high speed until of spreading consistency. If it is too hard, add a few drops of water; if it sets up too quickly, return it to the heat to soften up.

Yield: 3 cups

The soul of a caramel cake is, of course, the icing. And in Columbus, Mississippi, no one is more renowned for her caramel icing than Mrs. Cora Mae Harris. Mrs. Harris has been making and selling her caramel cakes to folks around Columbus for ages. While we can't swear that this cake recipe is one that she ever used, the icing is all hers. Thank you, Mrs. Harris; now we can all enjoy "your" caramel cakes for generations to come.

Carrot Cake

1 1/4 cups canola oil
2 cups sugar
4 eggs
2 cups sifted all-purpose flour
2 teaspoons baking soda
1 teaspoon salt
1 tablespoon cinnamon
2 teaspoons vanilla extract
3 cups shredded carrots
1/2 cup (1 stick) butter, softened
8 ounces cream cheese, softened
1 (1-pound) package confectioners' sugar
1 cup chopped nuts

Mix the canola oil and sugar in a large bowl. Add the eggs 1 at a time, beating well after each addition. Mix the flour, baking soda and salt in a bowl. Add to the sugar mixture. Stir to mix well. Stir in the cinnamon and vanilla. Add the carrots and mix well. Divide the batter between 3 greased and floured 9-inch cake pans. Bake at 325 degrees for 30 minutes or until a wooden pick inserted in the center comes out clean. Cool in the pans for 10 minutes. Remove to a wire rack to cool completely.

Mix the butter, cream cheese and confectioners' sugar in a bowl until smooth. Stir in the nuts. Spread between the layers and over the top and side of the cake. Cover and chill.

Yield: 12 servings

Chocolate Birthday Cake

1 cup (2 sticks) butter, softened
$1/2$ cup shortening
3 cups sugar
5 eggs
3 cups cake flour
$1/2$ cup baking cocoa
$1/2$ teaspoon baking powder
$1/4$ teaspoon salt
$1^1/4$ cups milk
1 tablespoon vanilla extract
$1/2$ cup (1 stick) butter
$1/4$ cup baking cocoa
6 tablespoons milk
1 (1-pound) package confectioners' sugar, sifted

Beat 1 cup butter and the shortening in a large mixing bowl until light and fluffy. Beat in the sugar. Add the eggs 1 at a time, beating well after each addition. Sift the flour, $1/2$ cup baking cocoa, baking powder and salt into a bowl. Beat the dry ingredients and $1^1/4$ cups milk alternately into the batter. Beat in the vanilla. Pour the batter into a greased and floured tube pan. Bake at 325 degrees for $1^1/4$ hours or until a wooden pick inserted in the center comes out clean. Cool in the pan for 10 minutes. Invert onto a serving plate.

Combine $1/2$ cup butter, $1/4$ cup baking cocoa and 6 tablespoons milk in a saucepan. Bring to a boil. Remove from the heat and beat in the confectioners' sugar. Pour over the cake while still warm. You may add chopped pecans and miniature marshmallows for Rocky Road Icing.

Yield: 16 servings

Note:
The batter may be baked in 2 greased and floured 9-inch cake pans. Bake at 325 degrees for 25 to 30 minutes or until a wooden pick inserted in the center comes out clean. Spread the Rocky Road Icing between the layers and over the top and side of the cooled cake.

Fig Preserve Cake

2 cups all-purpose flour
$1/4$ teaspoon salt
1 teaspoon baking soda
$1^1/2$ cups sugar
1 teaspoon cinnamon
1 teaspoon nutmeg
$1/2$ teaspoon cloves
1 cup (2 sticks) butter, melted
3 eggs
1 cup buttermilk
11 ounces fig preserves, chopped
$1/2$ cup chopped pecans
1 teaspoon vanilla extract
$1/2$ cup sugar
$1/4$ cup buttermilk
1 tablespoon light corn syrup
$1/4$ cup ($1/2$ stick) butter
1 teaspoon vanilla extract
$1^1/2$ cups fig preserves, chopped

Sift the flour, salt, baking soda, $1^1/2$ cups sugar, cinnamon, nutmeg and cloves into a large bowl. Add 1 cup butter and beat well. Beat in the eggs. Add 1 cup buttermilk and beat until well mixed. Fold in 11 ounces fig preserves, the pecans and 1 teaspoon vanilla. Pour the batter into a greased 9×13-inch cake pan. Bake at 325 degrees for 45 to 60 minutes or until a wooden pick inserted in the center comes out clean. Remove the pan to a wire rack.

Combine $1/2$ cup sugar, $1/4$ cup buttermilk, the corn syrup and $1/4$ cup butter in a saucepan. Bring to a boil. Remove from the heat and stir in 1 teaspoon vanilla and $1^1/2$ cups fig preserves. Pour over the hot cake. Cool in the pan.

Yield: 15 servings

142

Italian Cream Cake

1 cup (2 sticks) butter, softened
2 cups sugar
$1/2$ teaspoon salt
1 teaspoon vanilla extract
5 large egg yolks
1 teaspoon baking soda
1 cup buttermilk
$2^1/4$ cups cake flour
5 large egg whites
1 cup toasted pecans, finely chopped
$1^1/3$ cups flaked coconut
$1/2$ cup (1 stick) butter, softened
8 ounces cream cheese, softened
1 (1-pound) package confectioners' sugar
1 teaspoon vanilla extract
1 cup toasted pecans, finely chopped

Cream 1 cup butter, the sugar, salt and 1 teaspoon vanilla in a large mixing bowl with an electric mixer until light and fluffy. Add the egg yolks 1 at a time, beating at medium speed for 30 seconds after each addition. Combine the baking soda and buttermilk in a bowl. Add the flour and buttermilk mixture alternately to the egg mixture, beginning and ending with the flour and beating well after each addition. Beat the egg whites in a mixing bowl until soft peaks form. Fold the egg whites into the batter. Fold in 1 cup toasted pecans and the coconut.

Divide the batter between 3 greased and floured 9-inch cake pans. Bake at 325 degrees for 35 to 40 minutes or until the layers pull away from the sides of the pans. Cool in the pans for 10 minutes. Remove to a wire rack to cool completely.

Beat $1/2$ cup butter, the cream cheese, confectioners' sugar and 1 teaspoon vanilla in a mixing bowl with an electric mixer until smooth and creamy. Fold in 1 cup toasted pecans. Spread between the layers and over the top and side of the cake. Serve at room temperature; refrigerate any leftovers.

Yield: 12 servings

Note:
To toast pecans, spread in a single layer on a baking sheet. Bake at 350 degrees for 8 to 10 minutes; let cool.

Texas Christmas Cake

1 pound golden raisins
1 cup whiskey
2 cups (4 sticks) butter, softened
2 cups sugar
6 egg yolks
4 cups cake flour
1 tablespoon baking powder
1 pound pecans, chopped
6 egg whites
Whiskey

Soak the raisins in 1 cup whiskey in a bowl. Cream the butter and sugar in a large mixing bowl until light and fluffy. Add the egg yolks 1 at a time, beating well after each addition. Stir in the raisin mixture. Mix the flour, baking powder and pecans in a bowl. Fold into the butter mixture.

Beat the egg whites in a mixing bowl until stiff peaks form. Fold into the batter until no white streaks remain. Pour into a well-greased tube pan.

Bake at 300 degrees for 2 1/2 hours or until a wooden pick inserted in the center comes out clean. Cool in the pan for 10 minutes. Remove to a wire rack to cool completely. Dampen a piece of cheesecloth with additional whiskey and wrap around the cake. Cover with plastic wrap. Let stand for 1 day before slicing.

Yield: 16 servings

"Hospitality is a gift of one's self to others."

Patty Roper
in Easy Hospitality

Red Velvet Cake

1/2 cup (1 stick) butter, softened
11/2 cups sugar
1 teaspoon vanilla extract
2 eggs
2 tablespoons baking cocoa
2 ounces liquid red food coloring
21/2 cups cake flour
1 teaspoon salt
1 cup buttermilk
1 tablespoon white vinegar
1 teaspoon baking soda
1 cup milk
5 tablespoons cake flour
1 cup (2 sticks) butter, softened
1 cup sugar
1 teaspoon vanilla extract

Cream 1/2 cup butter, 11/2 cups sugar and 1 teaspoon vanilla in a large mixing bowl until light and fluffy. Add the eggs 1 at a time, beating well after each addition. Mix the baking cocoa and food coloring in a small bowl to make a paste. Add to the egg mixture and beat well. Sift 21/2 cups flour and the salt into a bowl. Add the dry ingredients alternately with the buttermilk to the egg mixture, beginning and ending with the dry ingredients and beating well after each addition. Mix the vinegar and baking soda in a small bowl. Add to the batter and beat well. Pour into 3 well-greased 8-inch cake pans. Bake at 350 degrees for 20 to 30 minutes or until a wooden pick inserted in the center comes out clean. Cool in the pans for 10 minutes. Remove to a wire rack to cool completely.

Mix the cold milk and 5 tablespoons flour in a small saucepan. Bring to a simmer over medium heat. Cook until thickened, stirring constantly. Pour into a bowl. Chill until cool to the touch. Cream 1 cup butter, 1 cup sugar and 1 teaspoon vanilla in a mixing bowl until light and fluffy. Add to the cooled milk mixture and beat until smooth and fluffy. Spread between the layers and over the top and side of the cake.

Yield: 12 servings

Photograph for this recipe appears on page 134.

The origin of Red Velvet Cake goes back to the Waldorf-Astoria Hotel in New York, but Southerners have made it such a part of their holiday traditions for so long that it is now considered a Southern specialty. It is a beautifully textured chocolate cake that happens to be astonishingly red. The white icing is a startling contrast to the rich red cake. Red Velvet Cake has been a favorite with MUW students for decades and worth making two trips through the cafeteria line for that extra slice. Anyone who's seen the movie Steel Magnolias will remember the armadillo-shaped groom's cake with the blood-red interior. It had to be Red Velvet Cake!

Brown Velvet Cake

1 cup (2 sticks) butter, softened
2 1/2 cups sugar
4 egg yolks, well beaten
1/4 cup baking cocoa
1/4 cup strong brewed coffee
1 teaspoon baking soda
1/2 teaspoon baking powder
1 cup buttermilk
2 teaspoons vanilla extract
3 cups all-purpose flour
4 egg whites
1 cup (2 sticks) butter, softened
1 (2-pound) package confectioners' sugar
1/4 cup baking cocoa
1/4 cup strong brewed coffee
2 teaspoons vanilla extract
1 cup chopped nuts (optional)

Cream 1 cup butter and the sugar in a mixing bowl until light and fluffy. Beat in the egg yolks. Dissolve 1/4 cup baking cocoa in 1/4 cup coffee in a small bowl. Add to the egg mixture and beat well. Dissolve the baking soda and baking powder in the buttermilk in a bowl; stir in 2 teaspoons vanilla. Add the flour alternately with the buttermilk mixture to the egg mixture, beating well after each addition. Beat the egg whites in a mixing bowl until stiff peaks form. Fold into the batter. Divide between 3 greased 9-inch cake pans. Bake at 350 degrees for 25 to 30 minutes or until a wooden pick inserted in the center comes out clean. Cool in the pans for 5 minutes. Remove to a wire rack to cool completely.

Cream 1 cup butter and the confectioners' sugar in a mixing bowl until light and fluffy. Beat in 1/4 cup baking cocoa, 1/4 cup coffee, 2 teaspoons vanilla and the nuts. Add more confectioners' sugar or coffee to adjust the consistency. Spread between the layers and over the top and side of the cake.

Yield: 12 servings

Chocolate Mint Pound Cake

8 ounces sweet dark chocolate, chopped
1 cup (2 sticks) butter, softened
2 cups sugar
4 large eggs
3 cups sifted all-purpose flour
$1/2$ teaspoon baking soda
$1/4$ teaspoon salt
1 cup buttermilk
1 teaspoon vanilla extract
$1/2$ teaspoon mint extract
2 tablespoons water
1 tablespoon butter
1 tablespoon light corn syrup
2 tablespoons baking cocoa
1 cup confectioners' sugar
$1/2$ teaspoon mint extract

Place the chocolate in the top of a double boiler. Cook over simmering water until melted, stirring constantly. Remove from the heat and let cool slightly.

Cream 1 cup butter and the sugar in a large mixing bowl with an electric mixer until light and fluffy. Add the eggs 1 at a time, beating well after each addition. Mix the flour, baking soda and salt in a bowl. Combine the buttermilk, vanilla and $1/2$ teaspoon mint extract in a bowl. Add the dry ingredients alternately with the buttermilk mixture to the egg mixture, beginning and ending with the dry ingredients and beating well after each addition. Stir in the melted chocolate.

Pour into a well-greased tube pan. Bake at 300 degrees for 1 to $1^1/4$ hours or until a wooden pick inserted in the center comes out clean. Cool in the pan for 10 to 15 minutes. Remove to a wire rack to cool completely.

Combine the water, 1 tablespoon butter, corn syrup and baking cocoa in the top of a double boiler. Cook over hot water until melted and blended, stirring constantly. Add the confectioners' sugar and $1/2$ teaspoon mint extract and stir to mix well. Pour over the cake and let the glaze run down the side.

Yield: 16 to 20 servings

"Make new friends but keep the old. One is silver and the other gold." The Golden Girls of MUW remain loyal friends to their Alma Mater and to each other. Upon reaching their fiftieth reunion year, "W" alums are initiated into the Golden Girls. A luncheon is held in their honor at Homecoming, and the new inductees are presented with medallions.

Cream Cheese Pound Cake

3 cups sugar
1 cup (2 sticks) butter, softened
1/2 cup (1 stick) margarine, softened
8 ounces cream cheese, softened
6 large eggs
3 cups cake flour
1 tablespoon vanilla extract

Cream the sugar, butter, margarine and cream cheese in a large mixing bowl until light and fluffy. Add the eggs 1 at a time, beating well after each addition. Beat in the flour gradually. Add the vanilla and beat well. Pour the batter into a well-greased and lightly floured tube pan. Bake at 325 degrees for 80 to 90 minutes or until the cake tests done. Cool in the pan for 15 to 20 minutes. Remove to a wire rack to cool completely.

Yield: 16 to 20 servings

Graham Cracker Torte

(From MSCW Dining Hall, circa 1962)

3 egg whites
1/4 teaspoon cream of tartar
1/2 cup sugar
1/4 cup graham cracker crumbs
1 teaspoon baking powder
1/2 cup sugar
1/2 cup finely chopped almonds or pecans
1 teaspoon vanilla extract
1 cup whipping cream, whipped

Beat the egg whites and cream of tartar in a mixing bowl until stiff peaks form. Beat in 1/2 cup sugar gradually. Mix the graham cracker crumbs, baking powder and 1/2 cup sugar in a bowl. Fold into the egg white mixture. Fold in the almonds and vanilla. Spread in a buttered pie plate. Bake at 325 degrees for 25 to 30 minutes. Cool on a wire rack. Serve with the whipped cream.

Yield: 6 servings

Apple Custard Pie

2 unbaked (8-inch) pie shells
2 tablespoons butter
2 large Granny Smith apples, peeled, cored and thinly sliced
$1/4$ cup sugar
$1/2$ teaspoon cinnamon
3 eggs
$3/4$ cup sugar
4 cups scalded milk
1 teaspoon vanilla extract
Pinch of nutmeg

Bake the pie shells at 375 degrees for 10 minutes or until light brown. Remove to a wire rack to cool.

Melt the butter in a saucepan. Add the apples, $1/4$ cup sugar and cinnamon. Cook over medium-high heat for 10 minutes or until the apples are tender. Drain through a mesh strainer, pressing on the apples to remove all excess liquid. Divide the cooked apples between the 2 pie shells. Whisk the eggs and $3/4$ cup sugar in a bowl until fluffy. Whisk in the milk gradually. Whisk in the vanilla. Pour over the apples in the pie shells. Dust lightly with nutmeg. Bake at 325 degrees for 1 hour or until set. Remove to a wire rack to cool.

Yield: 12 to 16 servings

Banana Cream Pie

From MSCW Dining Hall, circa 1962

1/2 cup sugar
2 tablespoons cornstarch
$^1/_2$ teaspoon salt
3 egg yolks
2 cups scalded milk
1 tablespoon butter
$^1/_2$ teaspoon vanilla extract
3 ripe bananas, sliced
1 baked (9-inch) deep-dish pie shell
$^3/_4$ cup whipping cream, whipped

Mix the sugar, cornstarch and salt in a bowl. Add the egg yolks and mix well. Whisk in half the scalded milk. Combine with the remaining scalded milk in a saucepan. Cook until the custard boils and thickens, stirring constantly. Remove from the heat and stir in the butter and vanilla. Chill until cold.

Arrange a layer of banana slices in the baked pie shell. Top with the cold custard. Spread the whipped cream over the custard. Arrange a circle of banana slices around the edge, if desired. Refrigerate any leftovers.

Yield: 8 servings

Buttermilk Pie

1/2 cup (1 stick) butter, softened
11/2 cups sugar
3 eggs
2 tablespoons all-purpose flour
1/2 cup buttermilk
1 teaspoon vanilla extract
1 partially baked (9-inch) pie shell

Cream the butter and sugar in a mixing bowl until light and fluffy. Add the eggs and mix well. Whisk in the flour, buttermilk and vanilla. Pour into the partially baked pie shell. Bake at 350 degrees for 45 minutes or until golden brown and set. Remove to a wire rack to cool.

Yield: 6 servings

Chess Pie

3 eggs
51/3 tablespoons margarine, softened
11/2 cups sugar
1 tablespoon cornmeal
1 tablespoon white vinegar
1 teaspoon vanilla extract
Pinch of salt
1 unbaked (9-inch) pie shell

Cream the eggs and margarine in a mixing bowl until light and fluffy. Add the sugar, cornmeal, vinegar, vanilla and salt. Stir to mix well. Pour into the pie shell. Bake at 350 degrees for 30 to 40 minutes or until set. Remove to a wire rack to cool.

Yield: 6 to 8 servings

151

"When a Southerner leaves the South, he loses neither his accent nor his sense of place because he takes his cooking with him."

Betty Fussell
in I Hear America Cooking

Pumpkin Chess Pie

1/2 cup (1 stick) butter, softened
11/2 cups sugar
2 eggs
2 tablespoons all-purpose flour
1/2 teaspoon cinnamon
1/2 teaspoon nutmeg
1/2 teaspoon ginger
1/2 teaspoon allspice
1/4 teaspoon salt
1 (15-ounce) can pumpkin
3 tablespoons water
1 unbaked (9-inch) deep-dish pie shell
Whipped cream

Cream the butter and sugar in a mixing bowl until light and fluffy. Add the eggs and beat until light. Add the flour, cinnamon, nutmeg, ginger, allspice and salt. Stir to mix well. Fold in the pumpkin and water. Pour into the pie shell. Bake at 425 degrees for 15 minutes. Reduce the heat to 350 degrees and bake for 45 minutes. Remove to a wire rack to cool. Serve with whipped cream.

Yield: 8 servings

Easy Chocolate Chess Pie

1 1/2 cups sugar
3 tablespoons baking cocoa
1 teaspoon butter, melted
2 eggs, beaten
1 (5-ounce) can evaporated milk
1 teaspoon vanilla extract
1 unbaked (9-inch) pie shell
Whipped cream
Chocolate shavings

Mix the sugar and baking cocoa in a large bowl. Whisk the melted butter and eggs in a bowl. Add to the sugar mixture and stir well to mix. Stir in the evaporated milk and vanilla gradually. Pour into the pie shell. Bake at 325 degrees for 45 minutes or until golden brown and set. Remove to a wire rack to cool. Serve warm topped with whipped cream and chocolate shavings.

Yield: 6 to 8 servings

Easy Fudge Pie

1/2 cup (1 stick) butter, melted
6 tablespoons baking cocoa
2 eggs, lightly beaten
1 cup sugar
1 teaspoon vanilla extract
1/2 cup all-purpose flour
1 cup chopped nuts
Whipped cream or ice cream

Combine the melted butter and baking cocoa in a bowl. Stir until smooth. Add the eggs, sugar, vanilla, flour and nuts. Stir to mix well. Pour into a lightly buttered pie plate. Bake at 325 degrees for 20 to 25 minutes. Do not overbake; the texture should be fudgy. Remove to a wire rack to cool. Serve with whipped cream or ice cream.

Yield: 6 to 8 servings

"Southern ladies like to be gracious. Above all, they love to entertain. They love to make their home an inviting place and then invite people into it, make them feel comfortable, surrounded by lovely things, and feasting on delicious foods."

Phyllis Hoffman
Founder of Southern Lady Magazine

Homecoming may ordinarily conjure up images of fall and football, but MUW rolls out the red carpet for its alumnae every year in April, when the campus and the historic city of Columbus are wrapped in pink azaleas and purple wisteria vines. With fried chicken picnics, class reunions, concerts, and workshops, MUW's Homecoming celebration focuses on friends and food and leaves the football to everybody else.

Grape Tart

4 cups seedless grapes
2 baked (9-inch) tart shells in pans with removable bottoms
$^1/_2$ cup milk
$^1/_2$ cup heavy cream
2 large eggs
2 tablespoons Grand Marnier
$^1/_3$ cup sugar
1 teaspoon all-purpose flour
$^1/_2$ cup orange marmalade
2 tablespoons Grand Marnier

Divide the grapes between the 2 tart shells. Whisk the milk, cream, eggs, 2 tablespoons orange liqueur, sugar and flour in a bowl. Pour over the grapes. Place the tarts on baking sheets. Bake at 375 degrees for 20 to 25 minutes or until set. Remove the pans to a wire rack and let cool for 5 to 8 minutes. Loosen from the sides of the pans with a sharp knife and remove the sides. Heat the marmalade and 2 tablespoons orange liqueur in a small saucepan over low heat; strain. Brush the hot glaze over the tarts and serve warm.

Yield: 12 to 16 servings

Lemon Custard Pie

4 eggs
1$^1/_2$ cups sugar
Grated zest of 2 lemons
Juice of 2 lemons
6 tablespoons butter, melted
1 unbaked (9-inch) pie shell

Whisk the eggs, sugar, lemon zest, lemon juice and melted butter in a bowl. Pour into the pie shell. Bake at 325 degrees for 40 minutes. Remove to a wire rack to cool.

Yield: 6 to 8 servings

Peaches and Cream Pie

3/4 cup sugar
3 tablespoons cornstarch
1 cup boiling water
1 (3-ounce) package peach gelatin
2 cups sliced peeled fresh peaches
1 baked (9-inch) pie shell
1 cup whipping cream, whipped

Combine the sugar, cornstarch and boiling water in a saucepan. Cook over medium heat until the sugar and cornstarch dissolve. Whisk in the peach gelatin. Remove from the heat and let cool to lukewarm. Fold in the peaches and pour into the pie shell. Chill for 2 hours or until set. Top with the whipped cream before serving.

Yield: 6 to 8 servings

Peach and Blueberry Pie

1 1/4 cups sugar
1/4 cup quick-cooking tapioca
1 teaspoon finely grated lemon zest
1/2 teaspoon salt
2 tablespoons fresh lemon juice
3 cups sliced peeled peaches (about 6 large peaches)
1 cup fresh blueberries, rinsed and drained
1 (2-crust) pie pastry
Sugar

Mix 1 1/4 cups sugar, the tapioca, lemon zest and salt in a bowl. Sprinkle the lemon juice over the peaches and blueberries in a large bowl. Add the sugar mixture and toss gently to coat. Let stand for 15 to 20 minutes. Line a 9-inch deep-dish pie plate with 1 pie pastry. Spoon the filling into the crust. Fit the other pastry over the top. Flute the edges and cut slits to vent. Sprinkle with additional sugar. Bake at 400 degrees for 45 to 50 minutes or until golden brown.

Yield: 6 to 8 servings

155

"Miss Summerour, the school dietitian, held dining etiquette classes before the meals. She would stand in front of the room and show us the proper way to hold a knife and fork, where to put our napkins, and how to use a fingerbowl. This instruction and the inspiration of the beautiful table settings in the dining hall taught me to entertain graciously and to feel confident I was always doing the right thing. You go through life wanting white tablecloths and fresh flowers on your table!"

Carmen Pearson Ronkin
Class of 1937

Basic Pecan Pie

3/4 sugar
1 cup light corn syrup
3 eggs
1/2 cup (1 stick) butter, softened
1 tablespoon all-purpose flour
1 teaspoon vanilla extract
1 unbaked (9-inch) pie shell
1 1/2 cups pecan halves

Beat the sugar, corn syrup, eggs, butter, flour and vanilla in a mixing bowl with an electric mixer at medium speed for 12 minutes. Pour into the pie shell and arrange the pecans in concentric circles on top. Bake at 350 degrees for 1 hour or until set and golden brown. Remove to a wire rack to cool.

Yield: 8 servings

Variation:
Add 2 tablespoons bourbon to the filling for a Kentucky Pecan Pie.

"W" Praline Delight Pie

6 tablespoon butter, melted
1/2 cup packed brown sugar
1/2 cup chopped nuts
1 baked (9-inch) pie shell
3/4 cup sugar
1/2 teaspoon salt
5 tablespoons cornstarch
2 2/3 cups warm water
1 1/4 cups powdered milk
5 egg yolks, beaten
1 tablespoon butter
3/4 teaspoon vanilla extract
1 2/3 cups whipping cream, whipped
1/4 cup chopped nuts

Mix the melted butter, brown sugar and 1/2 cup nuts in a bowl.
Spread in the pie shell. Bake at 425 degrees for 5 minutes or until
bubbly. Remove to a wire rack and let cool.

Mix the sugar, salt, cornstarch, warm water and powdered
milk in a saucepan. Whisk in the egg yolks. Cook over medium
heat until boiling and thickened, stirring frequently. Cook for
10 minutes longer. Remove from the heat and stir in 1 tablespoon
butter and the vanilla. Chill in the saucepan until cold. Pour into
the pie shell. Top with the whipped cream and sprinkle with
1/4 cup chopped nuts.

Yield: 6 to 8 servings

Mary Wilson Home Sweet Potato Pie

1¹/2 cups mashed cooked sweet potatoes
2 eggs, beaten
¹/2 cup packed brown sugar
1 teaspoon cinnamon
1 teaspoon ginger
1¹/2 cups scalded milk
¹/4 teaspoon salt
1 unbaked (9-inch) pie shell
¹/4 cup (¹/2 stick) butter, softened
¹/2 cup packed brown sugar
¹/4 cup chopped pecans

Combine the mashed sweet potatoes, eggs, ¹/2 cup brown sugar, cinnamon, ginger, scalded milk and salt in a bowl. Stir to mix well. Pour into the pie shell. Mix the butter, ¹/2 cup brown sugar and pecans in a bowl. Sprinkle over the filling. Place the pie on a baking sheet. Bake at 350 degrees for 20 minutes or until almost set. Remove to a wire rack to cool.

Yield: 6 to 8 servings

Mother's Never-Fail Piecrust

3 cups all-purpose flour
1 teaspoon salt
1 cup shortening
2 tablespoons cold water
1 tablespoon vinegar
1 egg

Combine the flour and salt in a bowl. Cut in the shortening with a pastry blender or fork until it resembles small peas. Mix the cold water, vinegar and egg in a small bowl. Stir into the flour mixture gradually. Knead the dough gently on a floured work surface for a short time. Divide the dough into 3 balls. Roll out on a lightly floured surface. Fit into the bottoms of three 9-inch pie plates. Bake at 450 degrees for 8 to 10 minutes.

Yield: 3 (1-crust) pie pastries

Version 2

3 cups all-purpose flour
1 teaspoon salt
1/3 cup shortening
3 tablespoons cold water

Combine the flour and salt in a bowl. Cut in the shortening with a pastry blender or fork until it resembles small peas. Stir the cold water into the flour mixture gradually. Knead the dough gently on a floured work surface for a short time. Divide the dough into 3 balls. Roll out on a lightly floured surface. Fit into the bottoms of three 9-inch pie plates. Bake at 450 degrees for 8 to 10 minutes.

Yield: 3 (1-crust) pie pastries

Graham Cracker Crust

Combine 1 1/2 cups graham cracker crumbs, 1/2 cup sugar, 1/2 cup (1 stick) melted butter and 1 teaspoon cinnamon in a bowl. Mix with a fork. Press the crumbs into a 10-inch pie plate, using the bottom of a flat cup to press firmly. Chill for 10 minutes.

Baked Apples with Cranberries

Zest of 1 orange, chopped
4 cups water
4 Rome or Golden Delicious apples
2 cups fresh cranberries
Juice of 2 oranges
1/4 cup packed brown sugar
1 tablespoon butter, melted
4 cinnamon sticks

Combine the orange zest and water in a saucepan. Bring to a boil. Cook for 10 minutes; drain and discard the cooking water.

Slice 1/4 inch off the top of each apple. Cut out the stem, leaving a small hole. Set the caps aside. Core the center of each apple with a melon ball cutter, leaving a 1-inch-wide cavity. Stand the apples in a baking dish.

Combine the cranberries, cooked orange zest, orange juice, brown sugar and melted butter in a bowl. Toss to mix. Fill the apple cavities with half the cranberry mixture. Spoon the remaining cranberry mixture around the apples in the baking dish. Place a cinnamon stick through the hole in each apple cap and place on top of the filled apples.

Bake at 400 degrees for 30 to 40 minutes. Serve as a dessert with ice cream or whipped cream or as a side dish with roast pork or turkey.

Yield: 4 servings

Apple Crisp

8 Granny Smith apples, peeled, cored and sliced
1 1/2 cups sugar
1 cup all-purpose flour
1 teaspoon cinnamon
1 teaspoon nutmeg
1/2 cup (1 stick) butter
Whipped cream or ice cream (optional)

Arrange the apple slices in an even layer in a buttered 9×13-inch baking dish. Sift the sugar, flour, cinnamon and nutmeg into a bowl. Cut in the butter with a pastry blender or fork until crumbly. Sprinkle over the apples. Bake at 375 degrees for 45 minutes or until the apples are tender and the topping is golden brown. Remove to a wire rack to cool slightly. Serve hot with whipped cream or ice cream.

Yield: 10 to 12 servings

Berry Compote

3 cups assorted fresh berries such as raspberries, blueberries, strawberries and blackberries
1/2 cup sugar
Juice of 2 oranges
Grated zest of 1 orange
1/4 cup honey
1 cinnamon stick
3 tablespoons brandy

Combine the berries, sugar and orange juice in a nonreactive saucepan. Bring to a simmer over low heat. Cook until the fruit is soft but still intact. Strain the fruit, reserving the liquid. Set the fruit aside and return the liquid to the saucepan. Add the orange zest, honey, cinnamon stick and brandy to the saucepan. Bring to a boil. Cook until reduced and thickened. Remove from the heat and let cool to room temperature. Fold in the berries. Cover and chill. Serve with pound cake or ice cream.

Yield: 2 cups

West Point may have its Long Gray Line, but The W has its Long Blue Line. The term "Long Blue Line" refers to the unbroken line of loyal and supportive "W" alumni that stretches back though the decades. The term probably refers to the navy blue uniforms worn from the inception of the school in 1884 until 1945, when the student body voted to discontinue the school uniform requirement. The Long Blue Line March is part of the annual Homecoming celebration, as alumni march into convocation in order of their graduation year.

Peach Cobbler

$1/2$ cup sugar
$1/4$ cup water
2 tablespoons all-purpose flour
1 tablespoon lemon juice
$1/2$ teaspoon vanilla extract
$1/4$ teaspoon almond extract
$1/2$ teaspoon cinnamon
$1/4$ teaspoon salt
5 cups sliced peeled peaches (about 3 pounds)
2 tablespoons butter, cut into pieces
$1/2$ cup all-purpose flour
$1/2$ cup sugar
1 egg, beaten
2 tablespoons butter, softened
$1/2$ teaspoon baking powder
$1/4$ teaspoon salt

Mix $1/2$ cup sugar, the water, 2 tablespoons flour, lemon juice, vanilla, almond extract, cinnamon and $1/4$ teaspoon salt in a bowl. Add the peaches and toss to coat. Spoon into an 8×8-inch baking pan. Dot with the pieces of butter.

Combine $1/2$ cup flour, $1/2$ cup sugar, the egg, 2 tablespoons butter, baking powder and $1/4$ teaspoon salt in a bowl. Beat until smooth. Drop by spoonfuls evenly over the peach mixture. Bake at 375 degrees for 30 to 40 minutes or until the peaches are tender and the crust is golden brown.

Yield: 6 servings

Cheesecake

1 1/4 cups graham cracker crumbs or vanilla wafer crumbs
1/4 cup sugar
1/4 cup (1/2 stick) butter, melted
24 ounces cream cheese, softened
3/4 cup sugar
3 eggs
1 teaspoon grated lemon zest or lime zest
1 tablespoon lemon juice or lime juice
1 cup sour cream
2 tablespoons sugar
1 teaspoon vanilla extract

Mix the graham cracker crumbs and 1/4 cup sugar in a small bowl. Add the melted butter and stir to mix well. Press the crumbs into the bottom of a 9-inch springform pan, using the bottom of a flat cup to press firmly. Bake at 325 degrees for 10 minutes. Remove to a wire rack.

Beat the cream cheese and 3/4 cup sugar in a mixing bowl with an electric mixer until light and fluffy. Add the eggs 1 at a time, beating well after each addition. Add the lemon zest and lemon juice and beat until very smooth. Pour into the crust and bake at 300 degrees for 55 minutes.

Stir the sour cream, 2 tablespoons sugar and vanilla in a bowl until smooth. Pour evenly over the cheesecake. Bake for 10 minutes longer. Remove to a wire rack. Loosen from the side of the pan with a sharp knife and let cool completely before removing the side. Chill thoroughly. Serve with fruit.

Yield: 8 servings

*MUW Power Bars:
A Recipe for Alumnae
Participation*

Combine 1 cup students, 1 cup time, 1 cup marketing and 1 cup generous support and mix well. A warm sense of satisfaction will tell you when it is done!

For a tastier version of MUW "Power Bars," we recommend the following recipe. Mix 1/2 cup (1 stick) margarine, melted, and 1 1/2 cups crushed graham crackers in a bowl. Press in a jellyroll pan. Layer 1 cup (6 ounces) chocolate chips, 6 ounces butterscotch pieces, 4 ounces flaked coconut and 3/4 cup chopped walnuts in the order listed over the graham cracker layer. Pour one 14-ounce can sweetened condensed milk evenly over the layers. Bake at 350 degrees for about 30 minutes. Cool and cut into squares. The recipe makes about 40 squares. Enjoy with your friends!

Banana Praline Cheesecake

2 cups graham cracker crumbs
5 tablespoons unsalted butter, melted
1/4 cup packed light brown sugar
1 ripe banana, mashed
16 ounces cream cheese, softened
3/4 cup sugar
2 ripe bananas, mashed
3 tablespoons all-purpose flour
1/2 cup sour cream
3 large eggs
1/4 cup praline liqueur
1 cup packed dark brown sugar
1/4 cup (1/2 stick) unsalted butter
1/2 cup chopped pecans
1/4 cup praline liqueur
2 firm ripe bananas, sliced

Mix the graham cracker crumbs, 5 tablespoons butter, light brown sugar and 1 mashed banana in a bowl. Press onto the bottom and up the side of a 9-inch springform pan. Bake at 350 degrees for 5 minutes. Remove to a wire rack to cool.

Beat the cream cheese and sugar in a mixing bowl with an electric mixer at medium speed until light and fluffy. Beat in 2 mashed bananas, the flour and sour cream. Add the eggs 1 at a time, beating well after each addition. Scrape down the sides of the bowl frequently while beating. Add 1/4 cup praline liqueur and mix well. Pour into the prepared crust. Bake at 350 degrees for 50 to 55 minutes. Turn off the oven and leave the oven door ajar. Let the cheesecake stand in the oven for 30 minutes. Remove to a wire rack and let cool thoroughly. Loosen from the side of the pan with a sharp knife and remove the side.

Combine the dark brown sugar and 1/4 cup butter in a saucepan. Cook until melted and smooth. Stir in the pecans and 1/4 cup praline liqueur. Add the banana slices and stir gently. Pour over the top of the cheesecake or over individual servings.

Yield: 8 servings

164

Raspberry White Chocolate Crème Brûlée

  4 cups heavy cream
  6 ounces white chocolate, chopped
  10 egg yolks
  1/2 cup sugar
  2 teaspoons vanilla extract
  1 cup fresh or frozen raspberries
  3/4 cup packed brown sugar

Bring the cream to a simmer in a heavy saucepan. Remove from the heat and add the white chocolate. Stir until melted and smooth. Combine the egg yolks, sugar and vanilla in a bowl. Whisk 1 cup of the hot cream gradually into the egg yolks gradually. Whisk the warmed egg mixture back into the saucepan. Strain through a mesh strainer.

Divide the raspberries between twelve 4-ounce ramekins. Pour the custard into the ramekins. Place in a large baking pan. Add enough hot water to the pan to come halfway up the sides of the ramekins. Bake at 350 degrees for 50 to 55 minutes or until almost set. Remove the ramekins to a wire rack to cool. Cover and chill.

Sprinkle 1 tablespoon of the brown sugar over each custard. Place under a preheated broiler until the sugar melts.

Yield: 12 servings

"Each year as a fund-raiser, the Lowndes County Alumni Chapter has a Valentine's Extravaganza catered by The MUW Culinary Arts Institute. The year it was held in our home, Tuxedo Strawberries were served as a dessert selection. Plump and juicy strawberries were all dressed up in chocolate tuxedo vests, white chocolate shirts with tiny little chocolate buttons, and bow ties. After the event, CAI left a hostess gift of the delicious strawberries on our dining room table. It was cold in February, and these delicacies are best not refrigerated, but it would have been best not to forget about them for three days either. When I finally went into the dining room, you can imagine what a comical sight! Those macho strawberries had sprouted fuzzy "chest hair" that was peeping out of the tops of their little tuxedo shirts!"

Gail Ferguson Laws
Class of 1997
President,
MUW Alumnae Association

Bessie's Egg Custard

1 teaspoon all-purpose flour
3/4 cup sugar
3 eggs, beaten
1 1/2 cups milk
1 tablespoon butter, melted
1 teaspoon vanilla extract
1 unbaked (9-inch) pie shell

Mix the flour and sugar in a small bowl. Combine with the eggs in a bowl. Beat in the milk, melted butter and vanilla. Pour into the pie shell. Bake at 325 degrees for 45 to 60 minutes or until a knife inserted in the center comes out clean. Remove to a wire rack to cool.

Yield: 6 servings

Caramel Self-Saucing Pudding

1 cup lightly packed brown sugar
2 teaspoons cornmeal
1 1/2 cups boiling water
3 tablespoons butter, melted
1 cup self-rising flour
1/2 cup sugar
1/2 cup raisins, soaked in orange liqueur if desired
1/2 cup milk
1 teaspoon vanilla extract
Ice cream or whipped cream

Mix the brown sugar and cornmeal in a microwave-safe 2-quart or 8-inch square baking dish. Stir in the boiling water and butter. Microwave on High for 3 minutes, stirring once during cooking. Sift the flour and sugar into a bowl. Stir in the raisins, milk and vanilla. Drop by tablespoonfuls onto the hot caramel sauce. Bake at 350 degrees for 35 minutes or until golden brown. Serve warm with ice cream or whipped cream.

Yield: 6 servings

Sugarplum Pudding

1 1/2 cups sugar
1 cup vegetable oil
3 eggs
2 cups all-purpose flour
1 teaspoon baking soda
1 teaspoon salt
1 teaspoon cinnamon
1 teaspoon nutmeg
1 teaspoon allspice
1 cup buttermilk
1 teaspoon vanilla extract
1 cup chopped cooked pitted unsweetened prunes
1 cup nuts, chopped
1 cup sugar
1/2 cup buttermilk
1/2 teaspoon baking soda
1 tablespoon light corn syrup
1/2 cup (1 stick) butter

Mix 1 1/2 cups sugar, the oil and eggs in a large bowl. Sift the flour, 1 teaspoon baking soda, salt, cinnamon, nutmeg and allspice into a bowl. Add the dry ingredients alternately with 1 cup buttermilk to the egg mixture, stirring well after each addition. Stir in the vanilla. Fold in the prunes and nuts.

Pour into a greased and floured 9×13-inch baking pan. Bake at 325 degrees for 40 to 60 minutes or until a wooden pick inserted in the center comes out clean. Remove to a wire rack and let cool slightly.

Combine 1 cup sugar, 1/2 cup buttermilk, 1/2 teaspoon baking soda, the corn syrup and butter in a saucepan. Cook for 10 to 15 minutes or until the sauce turns amber and begins to thicken, stirring frequently.

Poke holes in the surface of the warm cake with a fork or wooden pick. Pour the glaze over the hot cake gradually, allowing the glaze to soak into the cake. Allow the cake to cool completely. Cover and let stand for 24 hours for best flavor.

Yield: 15 servings

Rice Pudding

5 cups salted water
2 1/2 cups uncooked white rice
1/3 cup sugar
5 eggs, well beaten
1 2/3 cups sugar
4 cups milk
1 tablespoon vanilla extract
1/2 teaspoon salt
Dash of cinnamon
1 cup golden raisins

Bring the salted water to a boil in a saucepan. Add the rice and 1/3 cup sugar. Reduce the heat to low and cover. Simmer for 20 minutes or until the rice is tender. Beat the eggs, 1 2/3 cups sugar, milk, vanilla, salt and cinnamon in a bowl. Stir in the raisins and cooked rice.

Pour into a baking dish. Place the baking dish in a larger baking pan. Add hot water to the larger pan to a depth of 1 inch. Bake at 325 degrees for 1 1/2 hours. Remove to a wire rack to cool. Dust with cinnamon and nutmeg, if desired.

Yield: 8 to 10 servings

Carrot Soufflé

3 pounds carrots, sliced
1 1/2 cups (3 sticks) butter, softened
6 eggs
1/2 cup all-purpose flour
1 tablespoon baking powder
3 cups sugar
1/4 teaspoon nutmeg
1/4 teaspoon cardamom

Cook the carrots in boiling water in a covered saucepan for 15 minutes or until tender; drain. Combine the carrots, butter, eggs, flour, baking powder, sugar, nutmeg and cardamom in a food processor and process until smooth. Divide the mixture between 2 lightly greased 1 1/2-quart soufflé or baking dishes. Bake at 350 degrees for 1 hour or until set and light brown.

Yield: 12 servings

Boiled Custard Ice Cream

12 cups milk
6 eggs
6 cups sugar
6 tablespoons all-purpose flour or cornstarch
3 tablespoons vanilla extract
1/4 teaspoon salt

Bring the milk to a simmer in a heavy saucepan. Whisk the eggs, sugar and flour in a bowl. Whisk in a small amount of the hot milk. Return the warmed egg mixture to the hot milk gradually, stirring constantly. Cook until the custard coats the back of a spoon. Pour the custard into a bowl and set in an ice bath to cool. Stir in the vanilla and salt when cool. Cover and chill thoroughly. Freeze the mixture in an ice cream maker according to the manufacturer's directions.

Yield: 1 gallon

The first state-supported college for women in the United States was founded because of the untiring efforts of three determined Mississippi women: Sallie Eola Reneau, Annie Coleman Peyton, and Olivia Valentine Hastings. The faculty of the school consisted entirely of female professors until 1901, when the first male faculty member was hired. The original all-female faculty was led by Richard Watson Jones, the first president of the new school, and male presidents continued to lead the school until 1988, when Dr. Clyda Stokes Rent became the first female president of Mississippi University for Women.

Basic Ice Cream

8 cups milk
2 cups heavy cream
2 cups sugar
1/4 cup all-purpose flour
1/4 teaspoon salt
6 eggs
2 teaspoons vanilla extract or flavoring of your choice

Bring the milk and cream almost to a boil in a large saucepan. Mix the sugar, flour and salt in a bowl. Stir in enough of the hot milk mixture to make a creamy paste. Stir the paste into the hot milk in the saucepan. Bring to a boil and remove from the heat. Whisk the eggs in a bowl. Whisk 1 to 2 cups of the hot milk mixture into the eggs gradually. Return to the saucepan and whisk to mix well. Stir in the vanilla. Cover and chill thoroughly. Freeze the mixture in an ice cream maker according to the manufacturer's directions.

Yield: 1 gallon

Variations:
For *Coffee Ice Cream,* dissolve 1 tablespoon (or more) instant coffee granules in the hot milk. For *Chocolate Ice Cream,* increase the sugar to 2 1/2 cups, replace the flour with 1/4 cup baking cocoa and substitute 4 cups evaporated milk for the 4 cups regular milk. For *Fruit Ice Cream,* substitute 2 cups puréed fruit (such as strawberries, bananas or peaches) for 2 cups of the milk.

170

"*Snow started falling the day after I moved into the home economics home management apartment with 6 other girls. I was the cook that week and had done all the grocery shopping. We had just finished unpacking when we got word that classes had been canceled for the week. There we were in the penthouse apartment with a 19-inch color television (which was pretty good for 1977), plenty of food, and all the snow ice cream we could eat. Because of the snow, our professor, Dr. Savage, could not get to us and we certainly did not try to get out!*"

Jenny Katool
Class of 1978

Strawberry-Bourbon Ice Cream Sauce

1 cup packed brown sugar
1 cup sugar
1 cup water
1 cup strawberry preserves
Grated zest of 1 lemon
Juice of 1 lemon
1 cup pecan halves or walnut halves
1 orange, peeled, sectioned and cut into pieces
1/2 cup bourbon

Combine the brown sugar, sugar and water in a heavy saucepan. Bring to a boil. Cook until the mixture spins a thread, 226 degrees on a candy thermometer; do not stir. Add the strawberry preserves, lemon zest, lemon juice, pecans, orange pieces and bourbon and stir to mix. Remove from the heat and let cool. Pour into a covered food storage container. Store in the refrigerator.

Yield: 6 cups

Praline Ice Cream Sauce

1 1/2 cups packed light brown sugar
2/3 cup light corn syrup
1/4 cup (1/2 stick) butter
1 (5-ounce) can evaporated milk
1/2 cup chopped pecans

Combine the brown sugar, corn syrup and butter in a saucepan. Bring to a boil. Remove from the heat and let cool slightly. Stir in the evaporated milk and pecans. Store in the refrigerator.

Yield: 4 cups

Cookies and Candies

Looking toward Whitfield Hall from Puckett House

The Magnolia Chain

Perhaps the most charming of all "W" traditions is the Magnolia Chain, a ceremony held each May on the morning of graduation. "Though the distance may part us, our hearts will enshrine memories of days that are gone." Singing these words, seniors march two by two in cap and gown carrying a long chain of magnolias that has been made for them by the sophomore class. The magnolias for the 600-foot chain are gathered from the ancient trees at Friendship Cemetery and are a gift of love from the City of Columbus.

This custom has its origin in 1894, when graduates walked in line from the chapel carrying daisies as a part of commencement. Photographs from 1915 show graduates carrying a daisy chain, and in 1916 they carried a chain of magnolias. The ceremony consists of the class president's farewell address, the passing of campus offices to the junior class, the presentation of a class gift, and songs that have been part of the celebration for over one hundred years. After the Magnolia Chain ceremony is over, the seniors rush to the chain to claim a magnolia. Legend was that a girl who captured a blossom was certain to get a husband, and the tradition continues today as a prediction of good fortune.

Cherry Cheese Bars

1 1/4 cups all-purpose flour
1/2 cup packed brown sugar
1/2 cup (1 stick) butter
1/2 cup flaked coconut
1 cup finely chopped walnuts
8 ounces cream cheese, softened
1/3 cup sugar
1 egg
1 teaspoon vanilla extract
1 (30-ounce) can cherry pie filling

Mix the flour and brown sugar in a bowl. Cut in the butter with a pastry blender or fork until crumbly. Add the coconut and 1/2 cup of the walnuts and stir to mix well. Remove 1/2 cup of this mixture to a bowl and stir in the remaining 1/2 cup walnuts. Set aside to use for the topping. Press the remaining crumb mixture onto the bottom of 2 greased 8-inch square baking dishes or 1 greased 9×13-inch baking dish. Bake at 350 degrees for 12 to 15 minutes or until the edges are light brown.

Beat the cream cheese, sugar, egg and vanilla in a bowl until smooth. Spread over the hot crust. Bake at 350 degrees for 10 minutes. Spread the cherry pie filling on top of the cream cheese layer. Sprinkle with the reserved crumb topping. Bake for 15 minutes longer. Remove to a wire rack. Cut into bars when cool.

Yield: 32 bars

Photograph for this recipe appears on page 172.

Magnolia Chain Song

*To you, college comrades
     dear friends of our youth.
We tell of our love in our song
Though distance may part us
     our hearts will enshrine
Mem'ries of days that are gone.
Chain of magnolias we
     carry today,
Emblem of hopes and of fears
Its flowers may perish,
     its petals may fall,
But it binds us to you
     through the years.*

Frances O. Jones Gaither
Class of 1909

Chocolate Chip Butterscotch Bars

2 cups all-purpose flour
1/2 teaspoon baking soda
1 cup (2 sticks) butter, softened
1 cup packed light brown sugar
1 egg
2 teaspoons vanilla extract
1 cup chopped pecans
1 1/2 cups semisweet chocolate chips

Mix the flour and baking soda in a bowl. Cream the butter and brown sugar in a large mixing bowl with an electric mixer at medium speed until light and fluffy. Add the egg and vanilla and beat until smooth. Scrape down the side of the bowl.

Add the dry ingredients, pecans and chocolate chips. Beat at low speed just until combined; do not overmix. Spread evenly in a greased 8-inch square baking pan.

Bake at 300 degrees for 35 to 45 minutes or until a wooden pick inserted in the center comes out clean. Remove to a wire rack. Cut into 1×2-inch bars when cool.

Yield: 32 bars

Butterscotch Brownies

1/4 cup (1/2 stick) butter
1 cup butterscotch chips
1 cup packed light brown sugar
2 eggs
1/2 teaspoon vanilla extract
3/4 cup all-purpose flour
1 teaspoon baking powder
1/4 teaspoon salt
1/2 cup chopped nuts

Combine the butter and butterscotch chips in a saucepan. Cook until melted. Stir in the brown sugar. Remove the mixture to a bowl and let cool. Whisk in the eggs and vanilla. Sift the flour, baking powder and salt into a bowl. Stir into the egg mixture. Fold in the nuts. Spread in a greased 9×13-inch baking pan. Bake at 350 degrees for 25 minutes. Remove to a wire rack. Cut into 2-inch squares while warm.

Yield: 24 squares

"Southerners will forgive anybody anything if they have good manners."

Fannie Flagg

Chewy Chocolate Brownies

1 cup (2 sticks) butter
2 ounces bittersweet chocolate
2 cups sugar
2 eggs, beaten
1 cup all-purpose flour
1 cup chopped nuts
1 teaspoon vanilla extract
Confectioners' sugar

Melt the butter and chocolate in the top of a double boiler or in a heavy saucepan over low heat. Remove from the heat and let cool slightly. Stir in the sugar and eggs. Fold in the flour, nuts and vanilla. Spread in a greased 9×13-inch baking pan. Bake at 300 degrees for 45 minutes or until the brownies appear slightly undercooked. Remove to a wire rack and let cool for 1 hour. Cut into squares and dust with confectioners' sugar.

Yield: 24 squares

Almond Crunch Cookies

Fresh flowers on the dining tables at MUW were a tradition inspired by the campus gardens of Melissa Shattuck, Director of Housekeeping from 1896 to 1919. On May 11, 1952, The Columbus Dispatch reported that "Daisies tell of youth and love and kindred things. Every spring there comes a day, like yesterday, when nearly 100 white-covered tables in the dining hall of MSCW are centered with bowls of red roses and early blooming daisies. They make a pretty picture but they are a temptation. Nobody minds when the petals pile up because daisies do tell whether 'he loves me, or he loves me not.'"

1 cup sugar
1 cup confectioners' sugar
1 cup (2 sticks) butter, softened
1 cup vegetable oil
2 eggs
1 1/2 teaspoons almond extract
3 1/2 cups all-purpose flour
1 cup whole wheat flour
1 teaspoon baking soda
1 teaspoon salt
1 teaspoon cream of tartar
2 cups almonds, chopped
1 cup toffee bits
Sugar

Combine 1 cup sugar, the confectioners' sugar, butter and oil in a large mixing bowl. Beat with an electric mixer at medium speed until blended. Beat in the eggs and almond extract. Mix the all-purpose flour, whole wheat flour, baking soda, salt and cream of tartar in a bowl. Beat into the sugar mixture gradually, mixing just until combined. Stir in the almonds and toffee bits. Cover and chill for 3 hours.

Shape the dough into 1 1/2-inch balls and place 3 inches apart on ungreased cookie sheets. Flatten the cookies with a fork dipped in additional sugar, making a crisscross pattern. Bake at 350 degrees for 14 minutes or until light brown. Remove the cookies to a wire rack to cool.

Yield: 6 dozen cookies

Grandma's Butter Cookies

1 cup (2 sticks) butter, softened
1 cup sugar
2 egg yolks
Pinch of salt
$1^1/2$ teaspoons lemon extract
$2^1/2$ cups all-purpose flour
$1^1/2$ teaspoons baking soda
Sugar

Cream the butter and 1 cup sugar in a mixing bowl until light and fluffy. Beat in the egg yolks, salt and lemon extract. Combine the flour and baking soda in a bowl. Beat into the butter mixture. Shape the dough into walnut-size balls. Dip 1 side of the balls into additional sugar and place sugar side up on ungreased cookie sheets. Flatten the balls with a fork. Bake at 350 degrees for 8 to 10 minutes. Remove the cookies to a wire rack to cool.

Yield: 4 dozen cookies

Potato Chip Cookies

1 cup (2 sticks) butter, softened
$1/2$ cup sugar
$1/4$ teaspoon vanilla extract
2 cups all-purpose flour
$1/2$ cup each crushed plain potato chips and chopped pecans
Sugar
Confectioners' sugar (optional)

Beat the butter, $1/2$ cup sugar and vanilla in a mixing bowl until blended. Stir in the flour, potato chips and pecans. Cover and chill thoroughly. Shape the dough into teaspoon-size balls and place on ungreased cookie sheets. Dampen the bottom of a water glass with water and dip into additional sugar. Press the balls flat, reapplying water and sugar for each cookie. Bake at 350 degrees for 15 minutes or until golden brown. Roll the hot cookies in confectioners' sugar, if desired. Let cool on wire racks.

Yield: 3 dozen cookies

"My dear, this is something you must always remember. Your bosom can be fake. Your smile can be fake and your hair color can be fake. But your pearls and your silver must always be real."

Maryln Schwartz
Former Welty Weekend speaker, in A Southern Belle Primer

Caramel-Filled Chocolate Cookies

2^{1}/$_{2}$ cups all-purpose flour
^{3}/$_{4}$ cup baking cocoa
1 teaspoon baking soda
1 cup (2 sticks) butter, softened
1 cup packed brown sugar
1 cup sugar
2 eggs
2 teaspoons vanilla extract
48 soft caramel candies
^{1}/$_{2}$ cup finely chopped pecans
1 tablespoon sugar

Sift the flour, baking cocoa and baking soda into a bowl. Cream the butter, brown sugar and 1 cup sugar in a large mixing bowl until light and fluffy. Add the eggs and vanilla and beat well. Beat in the dry ingredients gradually.

Cover and chill for 30 minutes. Shape 1 tablespoon of the dough around each caramel candy, covering completely. Mix the pecans and 1 tablespoon sugar on a plate. Press 1 side of the balls into the pecan mixture and place coated side up on ungreased cookie sheets.

Bake at 375 degrees for 7 to 10 minutes or until set and slightly cracked. Cool on the cookie sheets for 2 minutes. Remove the cookies to a wire rack to cool completely.

Yield: 4 dozen cookies

Fudge Drop Cookies

1/4 cup (1/2 stick) butter, softened
1/2 cup sugar
1 egg
1/2 cup grape jelly
1 teaspoon vanilla extract
1 cup all-purpose flour
1/4 cup baking cocoa
2 teaspoons baking powder
2 cups walnuts, chopped
1 1/2 cups raisins
1 cup chocolate chips

Cream the butter and sugar in a mixing bowl until light and fluffy. Add the egg, grape jelly and vanilla and stir to mix well. Mix the flour, baking cocoa and baking powder in a bowl. Stir into the butter mixture. Stir in the walnuts, raisins and chocolate chips. Drop by rounded teaspoonfuls onto greased cookie sheets. Bake at 350 degrees for 10 minutes or until set. Remove the cookies to a wire rack to cool.

Yield: 4 dozen cookies

Chocolate Meringue Cookies

2 egg whites
Pinch of salt
3/4 cup sugar
1 teaspoon vanilla extract
1 cup semisweet chocolate chips
1 cup pecans, chopped

Beat the egg whites in a mixing bowl until foamy. Add the salt and beat in the sugar 1 tablespoon at a time. Beat until stiff peaks form. Fold in the vanilla, chocolate chips and pecans. Drop by teaspoonfuls onto foil-lined cookie sheets. Place in a 350-degree oven and turn off the heat. Let dry in the closed oven for 8 hours or overnight.

Yield: 3 dozen cookies

"When I was a freshman at The W in 1943, a friend and I decided to walk from the campus to town. We dressed according to the rules in our all-navy outfits, hats, gloves, and stockings and set out. As we walked along the street, a car pulled up beside us and a gentleman offered us a lift. We had been strictly warned that we were not allowed to accept rides from men so, of course, we declined the offer. We were surprised to discover later that the gentleman in question was Dr. Parkinson, President of MUW!"

Bess Moseley Cribbs
Class of 1947

Melting Moments

1 cup (2 sticks) butter, softened
3/4 cup sugar
1 cup (or more) all-purpose flour
1/2 teaspoon each baking powder and vinegar
Whole almonds

Cream the butter and sugar in a mixing bowl until light and fluffy. Mix in the flour, baking powder and vinegar. Stir in up to 1/2 cup more flour if the dough is too sticky. Drop by teaspoonfuls onto lightly greased cookie sheets. Press an almond on top of each cookie. Bake at 325 degrees for 15 to 18 minutes. Cool on a wire rack.

Yield: 5 dozen cookies

Photograph for this recipe appears on page 172.

Cinnamon Cookies

1 cup shortening
1 1/2 cups sugar
2 eggs
2 3/4 cups all-purpose flour
1 teaspoon each baking soda and cream of tartar
1/2 teaspoon salt
1 tablespoon cinnamon
2 tablespoons sugar
Maraschino cherries, halved

Cream the shortening and 1 1/2 cups sugar in a mixing bowl until light and fluffy. Add the eggs and beat well. Sift the flour, baking soda, cream of tartar and salt into a bowl. Add to the shortening mixture and beat well. Shape the dough into walnut-size balls. Mix the cinnamon and 2 tablespoons sugar in a bowl. Roll the balls in the cinnamon mixture to coat. Place on ungreased cookie sheets. Bake at 400 degrees for 10 minutes. Place a cherry half on each cookie. Bake for a few minutes longer or until golden brown. Remove the cookies to a wire rack to cool.

Yield: 3 to 4 dozen cookies

Nannie's Mincemeat Cookies

1 cup shortening
1¹/2 cups sugar
3 eggs
3 cups unsifted all-purpose flour
1 teaspoon baking soda
¹/2 teaspoon salt
1 teaspoon cinnamon
1 teaspoon allspice
1 teaspoon ground cloves
1 (9-ounce) package mincemeat, crumbled

Cream the shortening and sugar in a large mixing bowl with an electric mixer until light and fluffy. Add the eggs and beat until smooth. Mix the flour, baking soda, salt, cinnamon, allspice and cloves in a bowl. Beat gradually into the egg mixture. Stir in the mincemeat. Drop by rounded teaspoonfuls 2 inches apart onto greased cookie sheets. Bake at 350 degrees for 10 to 12 minutes or until light brown. Remove the cookies to a wire rack to cool.

Yield: 8 to 10 dozen cookies

Crispy Peanut Butter Cookies

1 cup creamy or chunky peanut butter
1 cup sugar
1 egg, beaten
1 teaspoon baking soda

Cream the peanut butter, sugar and egg in a mixing bowl until light and fluffy. Add the baking soda and mix well. Drop by teaspoonfuls onto ungreased cookie sheets. Make a crisscross pattern on each cookie with a fork dipped in water. Bake at 350 degrees for 8 to 10 minutes or until brown around the edges. Cool on the cookie sheets for 2 minutes. Remove the cookies to a wire rack to cool completely.

Yield: 2 dozen cookies

"Some of the juniors got it in our heads that we needed a Coke machine in our dorm basement. We marched to (MSCW President) Dr. Parkinson's office and made our plea. Without blinking, he said, 'No, not for our girls; it will bring in the lower element.'"

Opal Williams Wright
Class of 1951

Jumble Cookies

1 cup (2 sticks) butter, softened
1 cup sugar
1 cup packed brown sugar
2 eggs
1 teaspoon vanilla extract
2 cups all-purpose flour
1/2 teaspoon salt
1 teaspoon baking powder
1 teaspoon baking soda
2 cups rolled oats
1 cup crisp rice cereal or crushed cornflakes
1/2 cup flaked coconut
1/2 cup raisins
1/2 cup chopped pecans

Cream the butter, sugar, brown sugar, eggs and vanilla in a large mixing bowl until light and fluffy. Sift the flour, salt, baking powder and baking soda into a bowl. Add to the butter mixture and stir to mix well. Stir in the oats, cereal, coconut, raisins and pecans. Shape the dough into 2-inch balls and place 1 inch apart on lightly greased cookie sheets. Flatten the cookies with a fork. Bake at 350 degrees for 15 to 18 minutes. Remove the cookies to a wire rack to cool.

Yield: 5 dozen cookies

Moak's Oatmeal Coconut Cookies

1 cup butter-flavor shortening
1 cup sugar
1 cup packed brown sugar
2 eggs, lightly beaten
1 tablespoon almond extract
1 1/2 cups all-purpose flour
1 teaspoon salt
1 teaspoon baking soda
2 1/2 cups rolled oats
1 1/3 cups flaked coconut
1 to 2 cups chopped pecans or other nuts
1 cup raisins (optional)
All-purpose flour

Cream the shortening, sugar, brown sugar, eggs and almond extract in a large mixing bowl until light and fluffy. Sift 1 1/2 cups flour, the salt and baking soda into a bowl. Add to the shortening mixture and stir to mix well. Stir in the oats, coconut, pecans and raisins.

Drop by spoonfuls 1 inch apart onto parchment-lined or greased cookie sheets. Flatten the cookies with the back of a spoon dipped in additional flour.

Bake at 350 degrees for 13 minutes or until the edges are brown. Bake longer if crunchier cookies are desired. Remove the cookies to a wire rack to cool. Store in an airtight container or freeze.

Yield: 4 dozen cookies

Oatmeal Chocolate Chip Cookies

1 cup (2 sticks) butter, softened
1 cup sugar
1 cup packed brown sugar
2 eggs
1^1/$_2$ teaspoons vanilla extract
2^1/$_2$ cups rolled oats
2 cups all-purpose flour
^{1}/$_2$ teaspoon salt
1 teaspoon baking powder
1 teaspoon baking soda
1 (9-ounce) chocolate bar, grated
2 cups chocolate chips
1^1/$_2$ cups chopped nuts

Cream the butter, sugar and brown sugar in a large mixing bowl until light and fluffy.

Add the eggs and vanilla and stir to mix well. Grind the oats to a powder in a food processor or blender. Mix the ground oats, flour, salt, baking powder and baking soda in a bowl. Add to the butter mixture and stir to mix well. Stir in the grated chocolate, chocolate chips and nuts. Shape the dough into balls and place 2 inches apart on lightly greased cookie sheets. Bake at 375 degrees for 10 to 12 minutes. Remove the cookies to a wire rack to cool.

Yield: 5 dozen cookies

Refrigerator Cookies

1 cup shortening
1 cup sugar
1 cup packed brown sugar
1 teaspoon salt
2 eggs
3 cups all-purpose flour
1/2 teaspoon baking soda
1 teaspoon cinnamon
1 cup chopped nuts

Cream the shortening, sugar, brown sugar and salt in a large mixing bowl until light and fluffy. Add the eggs 1 at a time, mixing well after each addition. Mix the flour, baking soda, cinnamon and nuts in a bowl. Add to the shortening mixture and stir to mix well.

Divide the dough in half. Roll each half into a log on a floured work surface. Wrap in plastic wrap and chill. Cut into thin slices and place on nonstick cookie sheets. Bake at 375 degrees for 7 to 10 minutes or until golden brown. Remove the cookies to a wire rack to cool.

Yield: 6 dozen cookies

Thumbprint Cookies

1/2 cup (1 stick) butter, softened
1/4 cup packed brown sugar
1 egg yolk
1/2 teaspoon vanilla extract
1 cup flour, sifted
1/4 teaspoon salt
1 egg white, lightly beaten
Finely chopped pecans

Cream the butter, brown sugar, egg yolk and vanilla in a mixing bowl until light and fluffy. Mix the flour and salt in a bowl. Add to the butter mixture and stir to mix well.

Shape the dough into small balls. Dip each ball in the egg white and then roll in chopped pecans to coat. Place 1 inch apart on ungreased cookie sheets.

Bake at 350 degrees for 8 minutes. Press your thumb quickly but gently on top of each cookie. Bake for 8 minutes longer. Remove the cookies to a wire rack to cool.

Yield: 3 dozen cookies

Photograph for this recipe appears on page 172.

Modern-day etiquette consultants often tell their clients to eat before attending an important function, so they do not arrive hungry and embarrass themselves by eating everything in sight. Perhaps Margaret Mitchell was more to the point in Gone with the Wind *when she had Mammy tell Scarlett, "You can always tell a lady by that she eats like a bird."*

Miss Forbus' Date Balls

1 cup sugar
1 cup (2 sticks) butter
8 ounces pitted dates, chopped
1 cup chopped pecans
2 cups puffed rice cereal
Confectioners' sugar

Combine the sugar, butter and dates in a large saucepan. Bring to a boil. Cook for 8 minutes. Remove from the heat and let cool. Stir in the pecans. Combine the cereal and cooked date mixture in a large bowl. Stir to mix well. Shape into small balls and roll in confectioners' sugar.

Yield: 3 dozen balls

Chocolate Drops

$^1/_2$ cup (1 stick) butter
1 cup sugar
1 cup chunky peanut butter
$^1/_4$ cup baking cocoa
$^1/_2$ cup milk
3 cups rolled oats
$^1/_2$ teaspoon vanilla extract

Combine the butter, sugar, peanut butter, baking cocoa and milk in a saucepan. Bring to a boil. Cook for 2 minutes. Remove from the heat and stir in the oats and vanilla. Drop by teaspoonfuls onto buttered foil or waxed paper and let cool.

Yield: 4 dozen cookies

Therapeutic Fudge

2 cups sugar
$1/2$ teaspoon salt
3 tablespoons plus $1^1/2$ teaspoons baking cocoa
$3/4$ cup milk
1 tablespoon butter
1 tablespoon light corn syrup
1 teaspoon vanilla extract
2 tablespoons butter
$1/2$ cup chopped pecans or walnuts (optional)

Stir the sugar, salt and baking cocoa in a saucepan. Add the milk, 1 tablespoon butter and corn syrup and stir to mix well. Bring to a boil and reduce the heat to a slow continuous simmer. Cook to 240 degrees on a candy thermometer, soft-ball stage.

Remove from the heat and set in a sink containing 2 inches of cold water. Add the vanilla and 2 tablespoons butter. Stir slowly until the mixture is thick but still warm.

Remove the pan from the cool water. Stir quickly until the fudge begins to lose its gloss. Stir in the pecans and spread in a buttered 8-inch square pan. Let cool to room temperature and cut into squares.

Yield: 24 squares

Photograph for this recipe appears on page 172.

"My roommate and I went home every weekend and returned to campus on Sundays loaded with Mom-baked goodies to share. Anything not immediately consumed was left in our room for feasting during the week. We began to notice that someone was coming into our room every Monday and helping themselves to our hidden stash. We decided to catch the thief by adding Ex-lax to a batch of fudge. We then waited for the thief to be revealed. That evening, we heard someone ask if anyone had seen the housemother and the response, 'She is in her room. She has an upset stomach!'"

Patsy Lockhart McDaniel
Class of 1963
MUW Alumni Director

Microwave Caramel Corn

1/2 cup packed brown sugar
1/4 cup (1/2 stick) butter
2 tablespoons dark corn syrup
1/4 teaspoon salt
1/4 teaspoon baking soda
1/2 teaspoon vanilla extract
8 cups popped popcorn

Combine the brown sugar, butter, corn syrup and salt in a microwave-safe bowl. Microwave on High for 1 1/2 minutes; stir. Microwave on High for 2 1/2 minutes. Add the baking soda and vanilla and stir to mix well. Pour over the popcorn in a large microwave-safe bowl. Stir to coat evenly. Microwave on High for 2 minutes, stirring once halfway through cooking. Spread the caramel corn on a buttered baking sheet to cool.

Yield: 8 cups

Microwave Pralines

1 (1-pound) package light brown sugar
1 cup heavy cream
1 teaspoon butter
1 teaspoon vanilla extract
2 cups chopped pecans

Mix the brown sugar and cream in a 4-quart microwave-safe bowl. Microwave on High for 13 minutes. Stir in the butter and vanilla. Add the pecans and stir to mix well. Drop quickly by spoonfuls onto waxed paper and let cool.

Yield: 24 pralines

Note:
This makes a wonderful ice cream topping if it doesn't set.

The MUW "Symbol of Excellence" fountain, presented by the Class of 1967, has inscribed on it a quote from Alfred Lord Tennyson's "Ulysses," "Tis not too late to seek a newer world . . . To strive, to seek, to find, and not to yield."

Caramel Candy
From Industrial Institute & College, II&C

1/4 cup sugar
1 cup milk
2 tablespoons butter
2 cups sugar
1 cup chopped pecans or peanuts

Cook 1/4 cup sugar in a dry saucepan until melted and amber, stirring frequently. Add the milk, butter and 2 cups sugar. Cook to 240 degrees on a candy thermometer, soft-ball stage, stirring constantly. Remove from the heat and add the pecans. Beat until thickened. Pour into a buttered pan and let cool. Cut into squares.

Yield: 36 squares

Penuche
From Industrial Institute & College, II&C

2 cups packed brown sugar
3/4 cup milk
2 tablespoons butter
1/2 teaspoon vanilla extract
1 cup chopped nuts

Combine the brown sugar and milk in a saucepan. Cook over medium heat to 240 degrees on a candy thermometer, soft-ball stage, stirring constantly. Remove from the heat and add the butter, vanilla and nuts. Beat until thickened. Pour into a buttered pan and let cool. Cut into small squares.

Yield: 36 squares

Photograph for this recipe appears on page 172.

Microwave Peanut Brittle

1 cup raw peanuts
1 cup sugar
1/2 cup light corn syrup
1/4 to 1/2 teaspoon salt
1 teaspoon butter
1 teaspoon vanilla extract
1 teaspoon baking soda

Mix the peanuts, sugar, corn syrup and salt in a 1 1/2-quart microwave-safe bowl. Microwave on High for 7 to 8 minutes or until the peanuts are light brown, stirring well after 4 minutes. Stir in the butter and vanilla. Add the baking soda and stir to mix well. Pour the mixture onto a lightly greased baking sheet and let cool. Break into pieces when cool.

Yield: 1 pound

Note:
You may substitute roasted peanuts for the raw peanuts. Omit the salt and add the peanuts halfway though the cooking time.

"Men and women of Mississippi, you have a jewel! Preserve it!" This remark by Governor Robert Lowry during opening day ceremonies at II&C on October 22, 1885, is no less significant today than when it was first made. Mississippi University for Women has been a jewel in the crown of women's education for more than a century. It is the responsibility of us all to ensure that it continues to shine as brightly in the future.

Donors

Beth Buckley Aldridge

Libby Crouch Atkins

Avant Garde Salon

Myrrl Bean

Courtney Blossman

Katherine Crumpton Bryson

Marianne M. Cargo

Jessica C. Clarke

Collections

John and Eulalie Davis
in Memory of Florence McLeod Hazard '41

Jacqueline DiCicco

Betty Oliver Dill

Nutie Dowdle
in Memory of Alma Dowdle Conner

Alma Coign Ellis

Financial Concepts

Fannye Cox Franks

Hortense J. Gholson

Gifts, Etc.

Dr. Robert Gilbert

Ray and Trudy Gildea

Patti Harrison Griffin

Jo Neely Harper

Mary Ann Harrington

Cora Mae Harris

Rev. George "Tom" Hicks

Grayce Hicks

Mary Helen Hicks

Juanita McCown Hight

Margaret Bosarge Howell

Debbie Howland
in Honor of her mother, Betty Tate

Fran Ledyard Ivy

Helen B. Jenkins

Betty Clyde Jones

Betty Lou Stuart Jones

Beverly Koch Jones

Jay and Julie Jordan

Frances Spruill Jutman

Kathryn Roberts Leaken

Johnny Maloney

Patsy Lockhart McDaniel

Jean Norton

Andrea Godwin Overby

Bud and Joy Phillips of Belvedere Properties

Mary Ellen W. Pope

The Allen E. Puckett, Jr., Family
in Memory of Martha H. Puckett

Reeds of Columbus

Joyce Cade Sorrels

The Fitness Factor

Diane Vice, VIP Properties

Bettye H. Van Vulpen

Lillian Harris Wade

Mike and Betty Waters

Jean Pennington Wilder

Contributors

The Cookbook Committee wishes to thank the alumni and friends of Mississippi University for Women who shared their recipes and their memories of their days at The W.

Class Of	Name	Class Of	Name
1941	Elizabeth "Lib" Andress Ackerman	1940	Daysidel Day Bruister
1978	Pat Parish Acklin	1949	Katy Crumpton Bryson
1956	June Rowzee Addy	1972	Nancy Buchanan Bryson
1978	Beth Buckley Aldridge	1950	Dot Parks Buchanan
1970	Linda Alexander	1954	Peggy Beasley Cantelou
1958	Mary Geneva Ingram Allen	1954	Shirley Holland Carley
1960	Katherine Joyce Anderson	1978	Donna Lynnice Gentry Carter
1966	Barbara Bruce Applebaum	1933	Susie Lee Horton Chamberlain
2002	Augustus Argrett	1992	Holly McDaniel Church
1948	Helen Kelly Arnold	1943	Dollie Hughes Clark
1968	Libby Crouch Atkins	1984	Gwen Luke Clark
1961	Myrtle "Sisser" Goodin Austin	1956	Sylvia Duck Clark
1988	Camille Clark Ball	1951	Betty Lee Dance Coit
1938	Margueriette Spears Ball	2003	Leslee Colson
1973	Patricia Bassett Barck	1941	Martha Simmons Conerly
	Ann Clare Barr	1978	Robbin Archie Cox
1982	Lulu Ward Beall	1962	Ellen McMorrough Crawford
1961	Betty Brown Berry	1958	Sandra Bryan Crosthwait
1998	Kelli Caldwell Berry	1945	Annabelle Koonce Crowther
2003	Patricia Berry	1969	Linda Whitfield Crume
1964	Patricia Gartin Blair	1923	Jennie Hannah Crumpton
1945	Martha Evelyn Owens Booth	1974	Lynne Bryson Curtis
1946	Ada Carver Bounds	1975	Frances Daniel
1957	Fay Sanders Boyett	1990	Sallie Stockman Dawkins
1953	Bettie Davis Brandon	1947	Barbara Dean
1959	Dorothy Anne "Nonnie" Goodin Brink	1980	Susan Jane Dearing Dennis
1978	Rose B. Brook	1939	Helen Clark Dick
1980	Judy Brown	1955	Bobbie Fowler DuBard
2002	Sandra Walker Brown	1934	Emily Jones Duke
1945	Bonny Backstrom Bruce	1960	Janice Dunn

196	Class Of	Name	Class Of	Name
	1951	Irene Benton Eaves	1971	Nancy Mann Johnson
		Louise Edwards	1928	Annie Fay Jones
	1947	Margaret Boland Ellis		Margaret Joynt
	1954	Kim Alexander Farley	1999	Barry Karrh
	1996	Tiffany Sartain Flanders		Alfred Katool
	1962	Adelaide Williams Fletcher		Beatrice Katool
	1979	Lucy Rice Flowers	1978	Jennifer Katool
	1981	Katherine Franklin	1973	Sharon Simpson Kelso
	1930	Fannye Maude Cox Franks	1973	Pam Jones Key
	1973	Ricki Rayner Garrett		Meredith Kinsey
	1953	Pat Holloway Greer	1970	Sherry Keeton Konjura
		David Hampton	1997	Gail Ferguson Laws
	1972	Peggy Scott Hampton	1943	Dorothy (Dot) Stribling Main
	1970	Sonya Rye Hanson	1931	Allene McCormick
		Cora Mae Harris	1963	Patsy Lockhart McDaniel
	1963	Elizabeth Jemison Hawkins	1980	Mary Alice Birdsong McLaurin
	1952	Dolores Shankle Hazzlerigg	1938	Helen Luke McMahen
		Jean Heath	1985	Sheri Bennett-McMinn
	1976	Claudia Birdsong Henson	1968	Jan Wardlaw McSpadden
		Tom Hicks	1951	Dorothy (Dotty) Page Miller
	1934	Juanita McCown Hight	1944	Elizabeth Lawshe Miller
	1966	Gayle Harpe Hodge	1945	Juanita Cochran Miller
	1947	Martha Frances Medlin Holder	1964	Martha Jo Ballard Mims
	1968	Fran (Frances) Smith Houston	1984	Julie Addy Mitchell
	1951	Sarah Miller Howell	1971	Pink Nance Mize
	1965	Patricia Maxwell Hudgins	1971	Mary Jane Whitfield Moak
	1950	Nancy McClanahan Imes	1970	Carmen Cotton Montgomery
	1967	Faye Farish Iverlett	1995	Emily Myers
		Becky Jenkins	1961	Gabie Franks Nabors
	1954	Helen Byars Jenkins	1958	Marilyn McCaleb Neighbors

Contributors

continued

Class Of	Name	Class Of	Name
	Carol Newell	1947	Mary Ellen Rea Taylor
	Ralph Null		Jana L. Thompson
	Elizabeth Nyholm		Lacy M. Thompson
1947	Mary Mullins Oberlin	1968	Louann Dick Thompson
1988	Iris Crawley O'Brien	1963	Toni Underwood Thompson
1984	Hannah Bryson O'Brien	1950	Josephine Bennett Tierce
1969	Pam Rye Ott	1984	Karren Doll Tolliver
1952	Maggie Brumfield Parker	1960	Jane Moss Tyner
	Joy Phillips	1974	Kay Selby Vaughn
1980	Allison Archie Pittard	1996	Jennifer-Helyne (Jenah) Victor
1926	Mary Ellen Weathersby Pope		Diane Vice
1964	Ann Anderson Prince		Tonny Vice
1975	Susan Rayner Puckett	1970	Lynn Addkison Wagner
1987	Velda Harris Randle	1940	Dona Wilson Warshaw
1963	Wanda Gail Ray	2003	Lori Weathers
1961	Celeste Kemp Reed	1988	Rhonda Colburn Weeks
1955	Elaine Jernigan Reynolds	1991	Candy Goodgame Wheeler
1957	Carolyn Smithson Ritter	1953	Anne Robbins Whyte
1955	Lou Aust Robison	1931	Adele Smith Williams
1952	Lela Williams Rosenbaum		Karen A. Williams
	Mrs. John H. Scheidegger	1996	Sally Winstead Williams
1947	Joyce Cleveland Sellers	1949	Mildred Rea Witt
1957	Carole Sibley Smith	1944	Mary Sue Littlejohn Wonson
	Kim McDonald Smith	1978	Cissy Galloway Worley
1995	Mary Atkinson Smith		Marianne Wright
1955	Joyce Cade Sorrels	1953	Mary Patricia Sweatt Wright
1952	Allene Mitchell Springer	1948	Mary Peggy Bowie Yeatman
1963	Jeannette Barksdale Stockman	1976	Vivian Louque Yeatman
1973	Anne Swearingen	2000	Elizabeth Yoste
1930	Gabriella Lytle Taylor	1988	Missy Goodgame Younger

Index

Index

Index

Index

Index

Index

Index

Index

205

Southern Grace
Recipes and Remembrances from The W

Office of Alumni Relations
Mississippi University for Women
Post Office Box W-10
Columbus, Mississippi 39701
Toll free 877-462-8439 Ext. 7295
Fax 662-329-7466

Name

Street Address

City   State   Zip

Telephone

Your Order	Qty	Total
Southern Grace at $25.95 per book		$
Postage and handling at $4.50 for the first book and $1.00 for each additional book		$
Mississippi residents add 7% sales tax		$
	Total	$

Method of Payment: [   ] MasterCard   [   ] VISA

[   ] Check payable to Mississippi University for Women Alumnae Association

Account Number   Expiration Date

Cardholder Name

Signature

Photocopies will be accepted.